SECRET
BARNSTAPLE

Denise Holton and
Elizabeth Hammett

AMBERLEY

First published 2015

Amberley Publishing
The Hill, Stroud
Gloucestershire, GL5 4EP

www.amberley-books.com

ISBN 978 1 4456 4284 0 (print)
ISBN 978 1 4456 4297 0 (ebook)

British Library Cataloguing in Publication Data.
A catalogue record for this book is available from the
British Library.

Typesetting by Amberley Publishing.
Printed in Great Britain.

Contents

Introduction

The history of Barnstaple is a long and distinguished one, with much change over the centuries. It has been through good times and bad, and experienced prosperity and hardship, but it has remained the same in so many ways. Our aim in this book is to take you on a gentle tour of Barnstaple, and in the process inform and entertain the reader with facts about the town – some you may know, but hopefully many you may not.

The book is designed to be used as a guided walk around historic Barnstaple, with the book as your guide. The tour starts at Queen Anne's Walk – the beautiful Grade I listed, eighteenth-century colonnade, and continues around the town, taking in the many historic sites. The reader will discover the stories of the buildings and businesses, and the accounts of the people who lived and worked in them.

The story traditionally begins in 930 – the date in which Barnstaple claimed to have received its first charter. The basic layout of the town was already in place. Boutport Street and the High Street were in existence with a strong defensive wall surrounding the town.

Barnstaple was one of four 'burhs' and as such was allowed to mint coins. The earliest known coin made here dates back to King Eadwig's reign (955–59). The town was also an important centre of commerce. Its old name 'Bearde Staple' means the Market or Staple of Bearda. According to tradition, King Athelstan granted the town a charter with rights to hold markets and a fair.

By 1066, Barnstaple was a well-established town, and twenty years later was mentioned in the Domesday Book. The King held the Borough of Barnstaple for himself, and it was not until Henry I came to the throne that the first Lord of Barnstaple, Judhael of Totnes, was created. It was Judhael who, in 1107, founded the priory of St Mary Magdalene outside the town wall.

By 1290, Barnstaple had become an important trading centre, for wool in particular, and five years later sent two burgesses to represent the town in parliament.

The late sixteenth and early seventeenth centuries were the most exciting period in Barnstaple's development. The Great Quay was built at this time, leading to a great increase in trade. Tobacco was imported from the New World, and pottery, tools, cloth and other goods were exported in return. In 1603 work began on the building of a new quay, to cope with the expanding trade.

In 1642, the Civil War began. Barnstaple was first held by the Parliamentarians, but changed hands four times before the end of the war. After the war, Barnstaple settled down and established its position as a port and industrial centre, and in the eighteenth century Queen Anne's Walk was created in its present form as a merchants' exchange. Marshy land at the end of the bridge was drained and, in 1710, the first proposals were made to create a formal Square. Several roads leading to Barnstaple were repaired and widened after George III passed an act requiring this work to be carried out.

In 1825, steam was used for the first time in Barnstaple to power lace bobbins at the Derby Mill factory, and a year later the present guildhall was built, replacing the old guildhall (actually Barnstaple's second), which stood at the entrance to the churchyard. During the first half of the century, the population had doubled to 8,500, and by 1835 the town's boundaries were extended to include Pilton and Newport. There was much redesigning taking place and, in 1854, the Barnstaple–Exeter railway opened.

The continuing silting of the River Taw resulted in the running down of Barnstaple as a port, and, as time passed, the major part of the woollen industry moved to other parts of the country with other, larger ports taking much of Barnstaple's trade.

However, the twentieth century saw a gradual resurgence of Barnstaple's fortunes with several major firms settling in the town at Pottington and Roundswell. As we move further into a new century, Barnstaple continues to flourish as the chief town of North Devon.

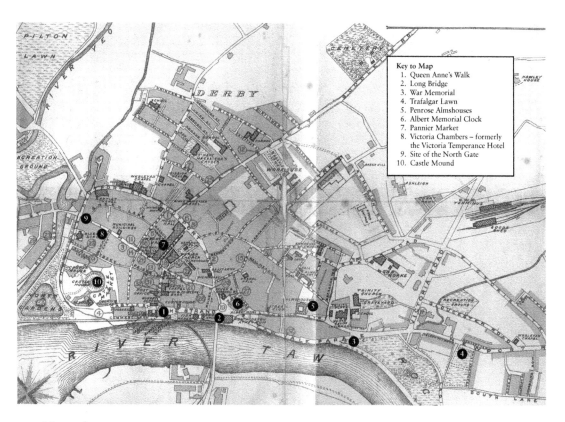

Key to Map
1. Queen Anne's Walk
2. Long Bridge
3. War Memorial
4. Trafalgar Lawn
5. Penrose Almshouses
6. Albert Memorial Clock
7. Pannier Market
8. Victoria Chambers – formerly the Victoria Temperance Hotel
9. Site of the North Gate
10. Castle Mound

Map *c.* 1895.

1. The Strand and The Long Bridge

Our historical walking tour of Barnstaple begins at Queen Anne's Walk on The Strand – now home to Barnstaple Heritage Centre. A merchant's walk or exchange has existed here since the seventeenth century, and early maps show the site standing alone jutting into the river. The prosperous merchants, who would spend their time here, all put money towards the building of a sheltered area to offer some protection from rain and wind when carrying out their business by the quay. The heraldic crests of those who contributed can be seen carved into the façade either side of the central statue of Queen

Queen Anne's Walk was the second merchants walk erected here.

Anne. The present structure dates from the early eighteenth century, but the columns may date from an earlier structure.

In 1859, Queen Anne's Walk was said to be rapidly falling into decay. Some entrepreneurs came to an agreement with the town council to erect some public baths and washhouses next to the Walk, as well as to refurbish the Queen Anne's Walk buildings. The completed work was officially inaugurated on Saturday 15 October when the mayor and around 100 dignitaries and local gentlemen paraded down Cross Street, led by a brass band. At the new building they sat at a long table and drank many toasts in port and sherry, including one to R. D. Gould who supervised the rebuilding.

They then marched back to the guildhall where the national anthem was played and cheers given for the mayor, who had also provided a cask of ale for the workmen and 'sent a half-dozen of wine to the station house for the use of the police, Beadles, etc.'

The Tome Stone was placed on the quay in 1633 to replace an earlier stone. Merchants would seal their bargains here by placing their money on the stone, agree a price and then shake hands before witnesses. Similar stones at Bristol and other places are called 'nails', hence the expression 'paying on the nail'. There are several names of merchants of that

The Tome Stone has been on this site since 1633.

The name of 'Delbridge' can be clearly seen engraved here.

time engraved around the edge of the stone, one in particular – John Delbridge – was one of the most well known of his age.

Delbridge was a Barnstaple man, trader, ship owner, mayor and Member of Parliament. His wife was the niece of Bishop Jewel, Bishop of Salisbury, but born at Berrynarbour and educated at Barnstaple Grammar School. His son, Richard, married Elizabeth Chichester from one of the landed families of the area. He was an important man not only in the history of Barnstaple but of the American colonies, and yet few in North Devon recognise his name. The reason for his obscurity probably has much to do with the date of his death – 1639 – with the country on the verge of civil war and normal life suspended. John Delbridge's surviving son died only two years after his father. His son-in-law, Martin Blake, who had been appointed vicar of Barnstaple at Delbridge's insistence, suffered under the commonwealth when he was ejected from his position. So by the time of the Restoration in 1660, when Blake was restored to his living, John Delbridge was already a distant memory. He was born in 1564 – six years into the reign of Elizabeth I and the same year as Shakespeare. This was the time when Barnstaple was growing and a time when those prepared to take risks could gain great rewards. Barnstaple was an important port, and the quay area was expanded and improved during these years. It is difficult to imagine now but the area outside what is now Queen Anne's Walk was the Great Quay and would have

The carved crest under Queen Anne showing the symbolic victories.

been constantly busy with ships loading and unloading, merchants making deals, sailors seeking work and, at times, with emigrants leaving England for a new life in the fledgling colonies.

Locally made cloth and pottery was exported and a wide variety of foreign goods imported, including wine, oranges and lemons, olive oil, raisins, almonds and anchovies. Adventurers and emigrants embarked for America and Australia; soldiers sailed to the wars in Ireland, France and the Netherlands.

Delbridge's father was a Barnstaple trader and, by 1591, John had started exporting and importing goods himself. He exported a coarse, cheap, worsted cloth called 'Barnstaple bayes'. He later became involved in the Newfoundland fishing trade. He became a member of the corporation and was mayor in 1600, 1615 and again in 1633. He took his responsibilities seriously, and when bad weather caused a scarcity of grain he was involved in securing supplies to save the poorer inhabitants of the town from starvation. He also restored the 'schoolhouse' – the grammar school housed since the Reformation in St Anne's chapel and where he had probably been educated. When in 1632 he retired to a property in Rumsam just outside Barnstaple, his house at the corner of Cross Street and High Street was rented out to provide a twice-yearly distribution of 1s to twenty poor families in Barnstaple.

This practical care is shown in the emigrant voyages in which he played a part. In 1620, his ship *The Swan* sailed to Virginia with seventy new settlers, not one of whom died on the voyage as was quite common on these perilous journeys. This was probably due

The Grenville family coat of arms on Queen Anne's Walk.

in part to John Delbridge's care in provisioning the ships well. Following the settlement in Bermuda, when a ship for Virginia was blown off course in 1609 and unexpectedly found the uninhabited island, Delbridge sent many ships and settlers there. These were profitable voyages for the new crop of tobacco that was grown there, and enormous quantities were imported to Barnstaple.

Not content with trading and colonisation, John Delbridge was also one of two Barnstaple MPs in parliament from 1610 for the next twenty years. He was also in direct contact with the Privy Council and Robert Cecil, Elizabeth I's chief minister, to whom Delbridge supplied information gained from his contacts and ship's voyages on the movements of the Spanish and French in various parts of the world.

It is sad that this man, who had such an influence on his time, is so largely forgotten now.

The statue of the reigning monarch Queen Anne, on top of Queen Anne's Walk, was given by Robert Rolle. The Rolle family had an influence on Barnstaple for centuries, although their main house was at Stevenstone near Torrington. The family's fortunes were founded by George Rolle – a successful Tudor lawyer who bought the Stevenstone estate in the 1520s. He later increased his wealth by dealing in the lands of Frithelstock, Pilton and Barnstaple priories. When he died he owned land in most of north and west Devon. In the following century, the family also acquired land in east Devon when, at the age of eleven, Denys Rolle succeeded to his grandfather's lands and also inherited his mother's lands at Bicton and Holcombe.

The headquarters of Barnstaple Voluntary Training Corps, The Strand.

During the Civil War, Sir Samuel Rolle raised a Parliamentarian regiment. There was an early and severe winter in 1645 and, although the Royalists were in control of Barnstaple, they were losing the war nationally. There was a shortage of coal in the area because the usual supply from Wales was cut off by a Parliamentarian squadron in the Bristol Channel. Sir Alan Apsley, Royalist Governor of Barnstaple, wrote to Edward Hyde, '...they having now stopped all our ships in Wales, soe that wee shalbe shortly undone for want of coals, did not Sir Samuel Rolles his woods growe so near us...' As he was on the other side the Royalists would have felt free to take anything they wanted from his land. Exactly where the woods were is unclear, but they may have been at Pottington, which was part of the Rolle estate.

Early in the following century, Robert Rolle gave the statue of Queen Anne to the town to be placed on top of the new merchant's walk, which became Queen Anne's Walk. In 1713, John Rolle became one of the town's MPs after paying off the town's debts. In 1739/40 Henry Rolle, the Recorder of Barnstaple, presented the corporation with portraits of the councillors, which still hang in the guildhall. In 1764, Denys Rolle gave a clock and bell to the Blue Coat School, which had been founded in 1710 at the North Gate. He was also one of the town's MPs. The clock can now be seen on the wall outside the guildhall.

Rolle Street and Rolle Quay are permanent reminders that this family once owned land in the town. In 1745, the lord of the manor of Pottington was said to be Mr Walter Rolle, 'in whose family as far as remembered'. There was then little at Pottington except marshland, but that changed after 1830 when Rolle Bridge was erected by the Braunton Turnpike Trust. The Rolles then constructed a quay with warehouses and industrial premises, and later there was residential development. By 1851 there were twenty-six dwellings, whose occupants included limeburners, millers, sawyers, mariners and ships' captains. In 1850, the timber merchant's firm of Rawle and Gammon (later Rawle, Gammon and Baker)

Looking down The Strand towards The Square and Bridge Chambers.

Bromley's Café along The Strand, remembered with affection by locals.

was founded on the site where they remained for over a century. In 1853, they started chartering their own vessels to import timber.

Lauder and Smith's brickmaking and drainage business began in 1876 when they leased land behind Rolle Quay where clay could be dug. By 1889, they had three kilns and between thirty and forty employees, but they ceased trading in the 1890s. In 1906, Barnstaple Town Council asked permission of the Hon. Mark Rolle to use the clay pits for refuse disposal.

Left: The view from the riverfront before the improvements took place.

Opposite: For many years, this was the shop of Thornby's confectioners.

In 1873, the Hon. Mark Rolle was the largest landowner in Devon in possession of 55,592 acres with a gross rental of £47,170 per annum. He was High Steward of Barnstaple, and his portrait hangs in the main chamber of the guildhall. He had two daughters but no sons, and after his death the Rolle estates passed to Lord Clinton.

Outside the heritage centre, set into a sunken area representing the Great Quay that once stood here, is the Millennium Mosaic. Constructed in the year 2000 as part of Barnstaple Millennium Celebrations, this imaginative piece takes the form of an 18-inch band approximately 33 feet in length with each panel showing a different chapter in the town's history. It was paid for by public subscription and sponsorship, and is a wonderful place to relax awhile during your day.

Leaving Queen Anne's Walk, step up to the riverbank and, turning left, head along towards the Long Bridge. On your left is the small building erected in 1922 as the bus station – now a café.

This structure replaced the old Quay station on the same site (1874–98) that had been built to accommodate the Barnstaple–Ilfracombe line. The trains had to cross the river from Junction Station, so a curved railway bridge was constructed. It left the west side of the River Taw just right of the Long Bridge and, curving at 90 degrees and 213 yards in length, joined the east side at this point. It comprised of fifteen pairs of main girders, each one 40 foot in length, with the weight of the bridge resting on wrought-iron piers sunk into the riverbed and filled with concrete. At its construction it had the tightest and shortest curve for a railway bridge in the world. It was demolished in 1977, but the iron struts where it was attached to the river wall can still be seen.

After passing the café, turn left and walk along the pavement to the road. Next turn right and you will pass Bridge Chambers. Next to Bridge Chambers there are some steep steps that lead down to the subway under the bridge, avoiding the traffic above.

DID YOU KNOW THAT...?

HIDDEN IN PLAIN SIGHT on the bridge is a representation of the Bridge Trust seal. It shows six arches of a bridge, and a chapel that refers to that of St Thomas, which used to stand at the town end of the bridge and a cross with a spread eagle in the centre. The chapel is believed to have been built by Henry de Tracey, who died around 1279. He was a distant relative of one of the murderers of Thomas Becket, which may explain why the chapel is dedicated to him.

The Long Bridge at Barnstaple has a very long history, but when it began is a mystery. Even before the existence of a bridge the river was crossed by a ford, probably downstream of the bridge near the end of Holland Street.

The first recorded reference to the bridge is in a document dated around 1280. The first recorded reference to it as the Long Bridge dates from 1303 when Alicia de Acklane granted 3d a year towards its upkeep. It is possible that the man responsible for its construction was Henry de Tracey, lord of the manor of Barnstaple for much of the thirteenth century. He was distantly related to William de Tracey, one of the murderers of Thomas Becket, and Henry built a chapel dedicated to the archbishop at the Barnstaple end of the bridge.

By 1437 the bridge (which may have been a timber decked structure) was clearly in a bad state of repair, as Bishop Lacy then granted indulgences to anyone contributing to its reconstruction. This bridge was referred to by Leland, writing in the middle of the following century, as 'the right great and sumptuous bridge of stone having sixteen high arches at Barnstaple'.

DID YOU KNOW THAT...?

In 1556 a licence was obtained from the Bishop of Exeter to employ collectors to solicit donations not only for the maintenance of the Long Bridge but also the causeways, which, it was said, ran for a quarter of a mile from each end of the bridge and had to be provided with 'long stones, posts and rails of timber'. During the course of roadworks in the early twentieth century, part of the causeway was revealed 4 feet below the surface. It was about 8 feet in width and formed of stones laid on edge which were well worn and had ruts caused by wheeled traffic.

It seems that three arches next to the Barnstaple bank, referred to as the 'Maiden Arches' were added or replaced during the sixteenth century. In his journal, Adam Wyatt noted that in 1589 'the arch cost XXVI pounds'. The exact nature of the work is unclear, as is the meaning of 'Maiden Arches'. It has been suggested that this is a corruption of 'midden' or rubbish dump, and may have been where the town sewer entered the river.

The width of the roadway on the medieval bridge was between 9 and 10 feet. At each end there were causeways to enable the traveller to gain access to the bridge. On the Barnstaple side the causeway went from the bridge to the beginning of High Street – the site of the South Gate. The river flowed over a much wider area then, especially at high tide. The Square was a marsh until it was drained in the early eighteenth century. In an article written for the Devonshire Association in 1946, Bruce Oliver calculated that the length of the bridge was 520 feet, the length of the town causeway was 300 feet and the length of Tawstock causeway was 1,500 feet. He also noted that he had seen part of the town causeway revealed by some roadworks, and it was about 4 feet below the

HIDDEN IN PLAIN SITE. The Bridge Trust crest in position.

road surface and about 8 feet wide. When at the end of the eighteenth century the Revd John Swete travelled to –Barnstaple from Tawstock, he noted the road 'brought me to Barnstaple, having [after the last descent] entered on the marshes, and passing on a mound raised above them crossed the River Taw on a fine bridge of fifteen arches, which connected them with the town ...'

Bridges were expensive structures to maintain and money was collected from a wide area for that purpose. In 1545, the mayor of Barnstaple authorized John Gerway to collect alms as far away as Dorset for the maintenance of the Long Bridge and causeway. He described the river as 'a great hugely mighty perilous and dreadful water'.

Many repairs and alterations have been carried out over the years. Between 1782 and 1807 the bridge was widened on the downstream side and, in 1834, on the upstream side, when cast iron railings replaced the existing parapets. In 1873, the London and South Western Railway obtained permission to divert the bridge at the Sticklepath side to make room for the railway bridge which would carry trains to Ilfracombe. The iron railings survived until the bridge was again widened to enable it to cope with modern traffic in 1961–63. It was at that time that responsibility for the bridge passed from the local Bridge Trust to the National Ministry for Transport.

Bridge Chambers and Bridge Buildings showing the distinct different styles.

Looking towards the Long Bridge, on the opposite side to the right the Shapland and Petter building, fine furniture makers (recently Leaderflush Shapland), can be seen. It was built in 1888 on the site of Westacott's second shipyard and was their second factory – the first at Raleigh having burnt down in March of that year, taking only three hours to be completely destroyed. Shapland and Petter began in the 1850s when Mr Shapland set up a business in a small portion of an old woollen mill in Raleigh. He was joined soon after by Mr Petter, who was a retired publisher and co-founder of the *North Devon Journal*. The business grew rapidly, and within a few years the firm acquired the entire Raleigh factory. By 1877, even this was too small and the firm purchased the Westacott site. They rapidly acquired a very high reputation for the quality of their work and had showrooms in Berners Street in London. A fine collection of their furniture can be seen in the Museum of Barnstaple and North Devon, and several pieces are still in place in the guildhall.

On the other side of the road to Bridge Chambers is the Museum of Barnstaple and North Devon. Built in 1872 by Mr Thorne as a private house, it became the Athenaeum in 1888 until this moved to the library buildings in Tuly Street.

The old bus
station built
in 1922 –
now a café.

DID YOU KNOW THAT...?

In August 1852 the *Lady Ebrington*, a clipper ship fitted out as an emigrant vessel, was launched at Barnstaple. The weather was fine, and it was said that there were more than 2,000 spectators assembled on the shore by 7.30 a.m. as she was towed down the river. A party of fifty or sixty ladies and gentlemen who boarded at the quay were treated to breakfast on board when she arrived at the pool between Appledore and Instow. She remained there for a few days before leaving for Liverpool, setting sail for Port Philip, Australia, in October of that year.

2. Taw Vale Parade, Rock Park and Newport

This fine Victorian thoroughfare was laid out in 1846 to improve the appearance of the town from the riverside. Prior to this, the houses along Litchdon Street backed straight down to the river. Taw Vale Parade proved to be a major undertaking as the entire riverbank had to be raised. The town council was very keen to improve the appearance of the town from the riverfront, and it was decided a better approach road from London and Exeter was needed. Shortly after construction, a grand terrace of houses was built to complete the effect. At a Town Council meeting, cllr G. K. Cotton insisted that a road should be opened up between Litchdon Street and Taw Vale Parade in case a fire broke out, so water could be brought from the beach straight to the affected area. It is worth noting the elegant bases to the lamp posts. Shaped like dolphins, they were installed in 1888. Marked Coalbrookdale, they were made at Abraham Darby's foundry in Shropshire.

Left: The obelisk in Rock Park, erected to commemorate the opening.

Opposite: The war memorial located in Rock Park, erected in 1922.

Taw Vale ends at the entrance to Rock Park, where the obelisk records the grand ceremony on 12 August 1979, when William Frederick Rock, the town's great Victorian benefactor, presented the deeds to the mayor.

DID YOU KNOW THAT...?

The lace factory at Newport has been largely forgotten. It was established in 1825 when Messrs Symonds & Co. leased land 'on the marsh nearly opposite the Infirmary on the Newport Road'. There was a lot of trouble with wilful damage and drunken employees. The construction of new limekilns led to flooding of the surrounding area, including the factory's engine house. In May 1837, all three of Barnstaple's lace factories were forced to close due to 'the state of the markets'. The other two factories soon reopened, but the one at Newport remained closed and was eventually demolished. The remains probably lie under Rock Park.

To create the Park, Mr Rock bought land to add to the existing area called Chanter's Green – formerly a marsh called Goose-lease, which had been dedicated to the public in 1863. It had required a great deal of determination and effort to acquire the land and turn it into a park. In a speech of 1886 praising Mr Rock, the mayor said,

> Persons of middle age might recollect the unsightly aspect, and indeed, unhealthy and unsavoury state of this portion of the town forty years since – the river above bridge almost inaccessible and quite shut out from view by limekilns and squalid buildings as far as a shipyard which formerly existed facing the Infirmary, from which point a marsh intersected with guts and open drains and occasionally overflowed by the tide, extended to Newport.

He went on to say that the improvement had commenced in 1845 with the removal of the limekilns and buildings and construction of Taw Vale Parade, which was opened in 1847. Many further improvements were made before the park was opened, including the removal of ruinous cottages, unsightly timber and brick yards, a limekiln and clay pit. Cooney Gut and other watercourses were drained and culverted, and nearly a mile of raised roadway was laid before the park could be laid out and planted. There were also complicated negotiations with the landowners, which delayed the process even further.

Street light along Taw Vale Parade showing the dolphin design.

On the day of dedication to the public, the mayor and councillors met at the guildhall and a procession was formed to walk to the park. It was headed by the band of the Royal North Devon Hussars and included schoolchildren, police officers, clergy and 'numbers of professional men, private gentlemen, tradesmen and other respectable inhabitants, walking two by two'. Thousands crowded into the park to witness the formal handing over of the deed of conveyance of the land by Mr Rock to the mayor.

The lodge at the entrance to the park was built to a design of R. D. Gould and financed by Mr Rock's brother-in-law and business partner, Mr Payne. He had married Prudence Rock and she furnished the lodge and also provided forty seats placed around the park. As well as accommodation for a park keeper, the lodge contained a room reserved as a shelter for ladies visiting the park.

Further on is the town's war memorial, which stands proud in a beautiful and well-kept flower garden. The war memorial was erected in 1922, with a solemn ceremony attended by the full council and local dignitaries. The families of those listed had pride of place at the ceremony and were each given a small booklet that had been published to commemorate the opening.

In the middle of the park, on a raised area that covered the remains of the limekiln, a bandstand was built to celebrate Queen Victoria's diamond jubilee. It was thatched in 1914, but was demolished in the 1960s. At the base of a tree near the site of the bandstand is a

The Lodge at the Newport Road entrance to Rock Park.

tree with a plaque almost hidden in its roots. It was planted by the mayoress in 1919 as part of the commemorations of the end of the First World War the previous year.

Continue walking through the park and you will see on the left the Millenary Stone – erected in 1930 as part of the celebrations of one thousand years of Barnstaple's history. Unfortunately the claim was based on a charter of King Aethelstan dated 930, which later research proved to be a forgery. There may not have been a charter, but clearly by 930 there was a settlement at Barnstaple. The town was sufficiently established to be granted the right to mint coins, the earliest surviving example of which is from the reign of King Eadwig (955–59). It seems to have been the least prolific of Devon's four Anglo-Saxon mints, with the greatest output during the reign of Aethlred II (973–1016). The mint finally ceased production in the 1120s.

As part of the millenary celebrations, a swimming pool was constructed on the land, but it closed many years ago and has now been demolished. *Walk back along the path, cross the road through the park (known as Ladies' Mile) and turn right up Park Lane, which leads to Newport.* Although it has obviously only been called 'Park' Lane since the existence of the park, it seems to be an old lane that has been known as Slymlane, Slimmey Land and Sandy Lane before becoming South Lane and then Park Lane. Possibly the earlier names are related to the path leading to limekilns behind the Stone.

In the high wall to the left is a gate through which Trafalgar Lawn can be glimpsed. The main entrance will be seen when walking back to the town down Newport Road. Continue to the top of the lane and turn left, passing Newport parish church. This is a building of the 1880s that largely replaced a building of 1829.

The Millenary Stone in Rock Park, erected in 1930.

Newport was established as a new town by the bishops of Exeter on their estate lands in the 1290s. It was part of the parish of Bishops Tawton until the municipal reforms of 1835/36, when both Newport and Pilton became part of Barnstaple (although Newport did not become a separate ecclesiastical parish until 1847). There was a medieval chapel near the present church, but it fell into disrepair and was described as 'ruinated' by 1630 – possibly because the roof caught fire. The chapel lands became The Newport Borough Lands administered by trustees. In 1654, Hugh Frayne rented the chapel and grounds as a dwelling house and garden. Later it became a barn, and in 1815 a cabinetmaker, William Oram, pulled it down and used the materials to make a house.

Medieval times were surprisingly violent. In 1383 the chaplain of Newport, Sir Richard ate Wood, was murdered by a father and son both named John Rassledge. They had property in Newport and Barnstaple, but the reason for the murder is unknown. They were excommunicated and the borough of Newport placed under an interdict for two years, during which no religious services were permitted.

Walk to the end of South Street and turn left, returning to the town centre down Newport Road. In 1912, the town council received a petition from the residents of Newport Road complaining of the speed of motors using that road and the dust arising therefrom. It was

On the corner of Gammon Lane, showing the early bricks.

resolved that notices be posted at the chief entrances to the town, requesting motorists to proceed slowly through the borough.

Although it had been founded as a new town with a market, fair, a mayor and other officials, it seems that it was not very successful. A deed of 1416 refers to the High Street of Newport Episcopi (for many years it was called this or the English version – Newport Bishop). In the seventeenth century, deeds sometimes referred to Middlestrete and Northstrete in Newport, but these road names do not appear to have stuck. A deed of 1792 refers to the Village of Newport, and refers to its main street as the Turnpike Road. In earlier centuries there was no direct route from Barnstaple to Newport, divided as it was by the Cooney water, sometimes called a stream but occasionally a river, and the marshes usually known as Goose-lease and Portmarsh. In 1320, The Bishop of Exeter and the mayor and commonalty of Barnstaple came to an agreement to build a mill or several fulling, corn and other mills on the Portemore stream – another name for the water that formed the boundary between their respective lands.

By the seventeenth century there was a causeway and bridge between Newport and Barnstaple. In 1801, William Oram was paid 'his bill for port and rails on Newport Cawsey

Holy Trinity churchyard. The church was built in 1845.

Member of
the Thornby
family, buried
in Holy Trinity
churchyard.

£556'. It is difficult now to realise how waterlogged Barnstaple and the adjoining areas were. The rivers and streams flowed in wider channels and were surrounded by marshes that were impassable at high tide. Even in 1853 one of the councillors remarked that he could remember when you had to walk ankle-deep in mud to get to Newport. Even The Square was not drained until the eighteenth century.

In 1796 Newport was referred to as a large village, and in 1830, Gribble, in his *Memorials of Barnstaple*, states, 'Cooney Gut a quarter of a mile on the London Road, and which runs between Barnstaple and the pleasant village of Newport'. The Newport Gate toll house of the turnpike road stood near the end of Union Terrace and was one of the most profitable, producing £681 in 1827, whereas the Bideford Gate made £158. Although the Turnpike Trusts did not end until around 1880, the tolls between Barnstaple and Newport and Pilton were ended much earlier.

DID YOU KNOW THAT...?

There were numerous problems with the customs service in the eighteenth centuy, as shown by the following notice from the London Gazette for 1706:

> Whereas THOMAS CLINTON, late Collector of the Customs for the Port of Barnstaple is withdrawn, and has been secreted from his relations by some who probably hope to acquire a considerable some of the Publick Money in his hands. These are to give notice that unless the said THOMAS CLINTON shall surrender himself ... the sum of Thirty pounds shall be given to any person that shall discover where he is ...

DID YOU KNOW THAT...?

Cotton, in his book the *Civil War in North Devon*, suggests that in 1646, when the Royalist governor of Barnstaple was preparing the defences of the town against an expected assault by the Parliamentarians, he broke down one or two arches of the bridge to cut off access from the other side of the river. Presumably because of that, a party of Royalist horses were posted at New Bridge near Bishops Tawton, where they were attacked and defeated, losing around eighty horses as well as baggage and troopers.

To the left as you walk down Newport Road a car park and flats called Congram's Close can be seen. Gribble, in 1830, states,

> The piece of ground (Congerham's) given by Alderman Appleby is now held by Mr William Thorne who took a lease of it in 1825 for sixty years, at £20 per annum ... the premises no longer consist of a field and ruinous mud-wall cottage, but exhibits six small respectable dwelling-houses and twenty-eight neat stone-built cottages, all with garden ground. These several buildings produce a rental of about £25 per annum.

In their turn these buildings fell into disrepair and have been replaced.

The Old Diary is remarkable for still being thatched, and is one of the few buildings to show signs of Newport's age. It probably began as a seventeenth-century farmhouse, becoming a dairy, a bakery and cafe before returning to private ownership.

In the late nineteenth and first half of the twentieth century, Newport flourished. Many new roads were built and there were many shops. The 1931 Kelly's Directory lists six dairies, four grocers, three confectioners and three butchers. There was a post office, three taxi-cab proprietors, a hairdresser, a blacksmith, two boot and shoe repairers, a newsagent, a fried fish shop, a music teacher and a school of dancing. There were two public houses

New Bus station, showing the town crest and mayor's crest.

(the Rose and Crown and the Rising Sun, the Rose and Crown has recently closed and is being coverted into cottages). Between 1937 and 1950 there was even a theatre called the John Gay Theatre, which is still fondly remembered by older inhabitants. For many years there was also a bank on the corner of Portland Street. This has now gone, along with the post office and the chemists.

On the left Trafalgar Lawn can be seen. This group of buildings was built by one of two prominent men with links to Nelson's navy, who settled in Barnstaple. Lewis Hole was born in 1779 and baptised at West Buckland, and his father was the Revd William Hole. Lewis Hole joined the navy at the age of fourteen, and by 1801 he was a lieutenant and served under Nelson at the Battle of Copenhagen. At Trafalgar he was First Lieutenant of the Revenge, and when the captain and commander were injured during the battle he took command of the ship. He was promoted to Commander for his bravery during the battle. He retired to Barnstaple at the end of hostilities, having made a substantial amount from prize money received through the capture of enemy ships. He lived at Ebberly Lawn, but decided to invest part of his fortune in building land. When he purchased the land that would become Trafalgar Lawn it was a large meadow known as Cowie or Coney Meadow and included what is now part of Rock Park. In August 1824 he placed an advertisement in the local paper for the sale of building land. When the buildings were finished, the largest became his residence and he died there in 1870 at the age of ninety-one. The situation of the land was described as 'healthy, agreeable and convenient' and promised that 'everything would be done to make this one of the most delightful spots in Devonshire'. During his retirement Lewis Hole was deeply involved in the numerous church organisations of the time, including the Church Missionary Society, the Church Pastoral Aid Society and the British and Foreign Bible Society.

Residents of Trafalgar Lawn included Mr and Mrs F. A. Jewell, who were mayor and mayoress of Barnstaple during the First World War. They had been marred at Newport parish Ccurch in 1891. Mrs Jewell was very active throughout the war in raising funds for Belgian refugees and many other charitable causes of the time. During the 1919 commemorations of the end of the war there were fireworks on the lawn.

Notice the post box in the wall of Trafalgar Lodge, which must be one of the oldest in Barnstaple as it is marked 'VR' for Victoria.

The other Trafalgar connection is Simon Gage Britton, who for twenty-five years was one of the surgeons at the North Devon Infirmary. Coincidentally, he is also connected with Newport. He lived for many years at King's Close in a house at the top of Newport on the Landkey Road. He was born in Bristol and studied surgery there. He qualified as first assistant surgeon (called surgeon's mate) and joined the navy, being appointed in

Once the base of street gas lamps, then a signpost.

The Shapland and Petter building, built in 1888.

1803 to the schooner *Pickle*. Later he passed his examinations as a surgeon, and in 1805 was appointed to the *Enchantress*. He apparently transferred to the *Victory* during the battle of Trafalgar, and may be included in the famous picture of the death of Nelson by A. W. Davis. His service with the navy ended when peace came in 1814. He became a general practitioner and worked for nine years in Bristol before moving to Barnstaple. He continued with general practice from his house for six years before becoming surgeon at the infirmary.

Just beyond Trafalgar Lawn is another reminder of that era in the group of houses known as Nelson Terrace.

On the opposite side of the road is Victoria Road, which has only been in existence since 1853. Beside that can be seen the stream just before it goes underground and eventually comes out to the river on the other side of the park. For many years Victoria Road was used for the annual cattle fair – part of the annual fair that is still held every year, although it no longer includes a cattle or horse fair.

Walk a short way along Victoria Road until you come to the entrance to the graveyard of Holy Trinity church. The gates are locked at night, but during the day it is possible to walk along the path and through the churchyard. Originally built in 1843–45, the church was rebuilt in 1868–70, apart from the tower. The other buildings were designed as a school with a large schoolroom at one end and a master's residence at the northern end. It continued to be used as a school until the 1960s.

South Street, Newport, showing the church.

The Long Bridge, taken from Rock Park.

3. Litchdon Street and The Square

Turn left when leaving the churchyard and on the corner you will see the modern Barum Court. This has been built on the site of the North Devon Infirmary, which served as the main hospital in the area from its construction in 1825, with Earl Fortescue having laid the foundation stone. £1,059 was raised by public subscription, with many more annual subscriptions promised from wealthy local benefactors. It opened to its first patients in August the following year and had twenty beds. In 1828 a wing was added for 'offensive or infectious patients', with further wings added in the following years. It finally closed in 1978 on the completion of the North Devon District hospital.

Until it became part of the NHS in 1948, the infirmary survived on subscriptions and donations. After the old hospital was demolished in 1983 the site was left empty for a few years to clear the air before a new building was begun.

Penrose Almshouses, Litchdon Street, erected in 1627.

Cross the road and walk down Litchdon Street which is one of the oldest streets in Barnstaple and was the main road out of town to London and Exeter. These provide a rare surviving example of seventeenth-century architecture in the town. The almshouses are a legacy of John Penrose, who was a local cloth merchant who died in 1624. In his will he directed that his executors were to buy 'some convenient place fit to erect an alms houses upon'. The inhabitants had to be from Barnstaple only and to be God fearing and non-drinking. There are twenty dwellings, each for two people, with a small garden plot at the back (now allotments). There is a chapel at one end and a meeting room at the other. The door of the meeting room has bullet holes, which were apparently the result of a skirmish during the Civil War. The cobbled courtyard with its water pump is visible from the street. The appearance of the almshouses has hardly changed over the centuries, although they have been modernised and brought up to date inside. The central entrance has granite pillars, and note the carved initials on the doorposts into the courtyard.

In the mid-1800s Dr Thomas Shephard Law, of Riverside Barnstaple, left £500 in his will, the proceeds of which were to be given in the form of coal to the inmates of the almshouses.

Above left: The musket holes in the door of the meeting room.

Above right: The original window glass and chimney in Penrose Almshouses.

As you pass the eighteenth-century Exeter Inn (now converted into houses), note the wide carriage entrance.

Further along the street you will see a door marked 'Entrance to the Pottery'. This refers to the old Brannam's Pottery. There was a working pottery here from at least 1830, and probably much earlier. Thomas Brannam bought the business in the 1850s, and his son, C. H. Brannam, commissioned local architect W. S. Oliver to build a new showroom with family accommodation. This was completed in 1886, with a second building for manufacturing the pottery added the following year. Further alterations were made in 1903 to leave the highly decorated façade now visible.

Thomas Brannam had concentrated on domestic earthenware and had exhibited at the Great Exhibition of 1851, which was when some of his sgraffito ware had been praised by Prince Albert. C. H. Brannam earned his reputation for his art pottery using highly decorated and exotic designs. In 1885, Queen Victoria ordered four large jardinières, and subsequently the pottery was known as 'Royal Barum Ware'. The cheque Brannams received for the purchase, signed by Queen Victoria herself, was never cashed but framed and hung on the wall of their showrooms for many years after.

Liberty's became Brannam's sole agent in London, and several members of the royal family bought pieces of the fashionable pottery. However, fashions change and by the time C. H. Brannam died in 1937, his factory was again concentrating on everyday household and garden pots, although special commemorative items continued to be made.

Once a coaching house, Exeter Inn has now been converted.

The firm moved to Roundswell Industrial Estate in 1989, mainly due to the impracticality of the old building. The large modern delivery lorries found it increasingly hard to manoeuvre along the narrow Litchdon Street entrance, with a policeman required to help direct traffic. Older residents of the street remember the chaos this would cause. A new open space was needed and the firm sadly moved.

One of the old bottle kilns was preserved when the pottery moved, which can be seen at the rear of the medical centre at the top of the narrow lane.

Return to Lichdon Street and continue walking towards The Square. Just two doors up from the pottery, at No. 8, it is worth noting the striking iron work at the upstairs window. This unusual and largely unnoticed piece is in the design of a clock, which perpetually states the time as 1.47.

Leaving Litchdon Street, you enter The Square. This is an area of Barnstaple that has been redesigned and changed more than any other. Almost every photograph or postcard taken of The Square shows a varying design or layout.

HIDDEN IN PLAIN SITE. Original Brannam's posters still in situ.

DID YOU KNOW THAT...?

In July 1872, Mr William Thorne's premises in The Square were undergoing extensive alterations prior to becoming a branch of the West of England and South Wales Banking Co. The same bank had occupied the premises about fifty years earlier before being transferred to Bridge Buildings. Previously the building had been the Greyhound Hotel. Mr Thorne was intending to move to his 'handsome, newly built mansion' on the other side of The Square, but he died a few months later and eventually that house became the Athenaeum. The house on the corner of The Square later became the Devon and Cornwall Bank.

Looking towards The Strand, notice two buildings either side of the road. On the right is Bridge Buildings, and to the left is Bridge Chambers. Both were designed by R. D. Gould, but show considerably different architectural styles. Bridge Buildings was built in 1844 in the fashionable Classical style. It was given a Stucco frontage with Greek Doric columns and Corinthian plasters, and a balustrated parapet followed the curve of the building from the Long Bridge and round to The Strand. A row of houses and a couple of public houses were demolished to build it. The block was continued to Maiden Street in the 1890s.

DID YOU KNOW THAT...?

Annie Hortense Youings and her husband bought Litchdon House in The Square. They enlarged it, and Annie Hortense and her two daughters ran it successfully as the Imperial Hotel. The daughters had been sent to cookery school, later managing the hotel kitchens. In September 1905, Princess Christian of Schleswig Holstein (Queen Victoria's third daughter, Helena) visited Barnstaple with her daughter and stayed at the Imperial. Upon seeing some blackberries in the market, the Princess requested that some be served at dinner that evening.

Bridge Chambers was built thirty years later in 1874 in the totally different Victorian Gothic style. The site had been occupied by a coal and culm store and the Ship Inn. Both premises were purchased by the town council for the sum of £650.

Richard Davie Gould was borough surveyor for fifty years and designed so many of Barnstaple's most prominent buildings that the *North Devon Journal* renamed Barnstaple 'Gould's Town' at one point in his career. As well as Bridge Buildings and Bridge Chambers, he also designed the Pannier Market, Butcher's Row, Taw Vale Parade, the

Congregational Jubilee Schoolrooms, Music Hall (now The Queen's Theatre), The bath and washhouse (behind Queen Anne's Walk), The North Devon Infirmary, Ebberley Lawn, the congregational church in Cross Street, the lay-out of Rock Park, 3–6 Castle Street and many more all around North Devon.

His family home was North Gate House in North Walk, though he later moved after his marriage to Pilton, and later again to Boutport Street. The council showed their appreciation of his long and distinguished career by awarding him a retirement allowance of £100 a year, but even as he lay ill in bed during his last months he still continued to work on designs, with the plans being spread out on his bed by his assistant.

His second son, Francis Carruthers Gould, became the famous political cartoonist and was the first of his kind to have a regular daily topical cartoon published in a national newspaper – *The Westminster Gazette.*

At the centrepiece of The Square stands the Albert Clock Tower. Built in 1862 by public subscription, it was the town's memorial to Prince Albert, husband of Queen Victoria,

Left: Brannam's bottle kiln, still in place in the medical centre.

Opposite: A piece of Brannam's pottery commemorative ware.

who had died the previous year. Originally the plan had been to erect a tower, but it was suggested that the town needed a clock, so the design was altered to accommodate this. A solemn ceremony took place at its opening, with the mayor and town dignitaries assembling at the base, and with the pendulum being set to start the clock at exactly 11.00 p.m. – the hour Prince Albert had died. The solemnity of the event was disturbed, however, by an extraordinary occurrence. A few days later it was reported extensively in the Journal that as the clock pendulum was started, with the drinking fountain beginning to flow at the same time, Mayor Norrington stepped forward to take the first drink. At this precise moment, an unknown person stepped forward and threw into the fountain 'about a teacup full of what his [Norrington] olfactory nerves soon convinced him was gin!' Norrington was a staunch teetotaller and was suitably horrified. He was quoted as saying that 'a great indignity was offered to the sovereign, to the memory of the illustrious prince, to the council, to the entire body of subscribers, and to the whole town'.

The Journal instigated a massive inquiry into who this man could be, with Norrington himself suggesting it must be 'some returned convict, some ticket-of-leave man, some poor ignorant and immoral wretch from the back slums?' In fact it later proved to be one John Baker, landlord of the Mermaid Inn and Tory town councillor, a fact which caused a sensation in the council chambers. There was an outcry for Baker to resign, with The Journal saying that 'Perhaps the ignoramus regarded his indecency as a joke?' Referring to the incident as 'a beastly outrage'. However, there is no record of John Baker having ever done such a thing.

The base of the clock tower has 'In memory of Albert Prince Consort, born 26 August 1819; died 14 December 1861' inscribed on the west side. On the east side it states:

HIDDEN IN PLAIN SITE. The wrought-iron clock, Litchdon Street.

This clock tower has been erected by the people of this town and neighbourhood to record their deep sense of loss the nation has sustained through the death of a good and wise Prince and counsellor, and also to express their loyalty to the Queen and sympathy with her in her great bereavement – John Norrington, Mayor.

The drinking fountain on the south side of the clock tower (no longer in use) was given by Sir William Fraser, MP. Fraser had stood for election as Barnstaple MP (the town at that point still returned two Members of Parliament) in the infamous 1852 election, where he and fellow politician Richard Bremridge had originally won the election, but were unseated after an inquiry. The electoral commissioners found that of the 696 voters who polled, 255 received bribes for their votes. One voter who summed up attitudes stated, 'I don't care who I vote for – hog, dog or devil.' The case was heard in the guildhall and was widely reported throughout the country. W. F. Gardiner, editor of the *North Devon Journal*, is quoted as saying, 'One cannot deal with the political history of Barnstaple with anything approaching pleasure.' A few years later, Bremridge stood for election again, this time winning on a fair vote. His grand and very large portrait now hangs proudly in the guildhall looking down on the place where he once stood trial. Incidentally, Benjamin Disraeli – later Prime Minister in 1868 and again in 1874–80 – was invited to stand as Conservative MP for Barnstaple in the early days of his career in 1837, but declined the offer.

The Albert Clock. Look closely to see the letter 'A's.

Near to the clock tower stands the fountain and bronze bust of Charles Sweet Willshire (mayor in 1876 and 1877).

The bust on The Square is that of local Liberal politician Charles Sweet Willshire and was paid for by his friends and erected four years after his death in 1889. Known during his lifetime as 'one of the most influential political leaders in the Western Counties', Willshire was the son of Thomas Lambe Willshire, owner of Newport Iron Foundry. Charles was his only son, and had shown an interest in politics from an early age. In 1852, when he was only fourteen, he went missing from home causing a search to be made. Eventually he was found in the Liberal committee room at Bath, having made his own way there to involve himself in the upcoming election. He was to become the youngest ever town councillor and went on to be the leader of the Liberal Party in North Devon, and mayor for a double term in 1876–77. Willshire was described as 'frank and honest, open as the day, bright as sunshine. As a politician he was a vigorous champion of advanced liberalism, and served his party with fidelity that never swerved and a courage that nothing seemed to daunt. To his opponents he proved an invincible foe – straight and hard hitter, yet generous withal.'

Willshire was a member of several Friendly Societies and sat as a local magistrate for many years. He had a reputation of being extremely fair and was known to pay the fines of those he considered in need of assistance.

It is remarkable that this local councillor was said to be Prime Minister Mr Gladstone's 'most trusted councillor' due to his honesty, unfailing support of the Liberal Party and his political skills. He developed ideas in connection with registration and organisation of local elections that were adopted by both the Liberal and Tory parties throughout the country.

When he died at the early age of fifty-two, his funeral was – and remains so – the biggest Barnstaple had ever seen. A procession started from his house in Taw Vale Parade, consisting of members of the local Liberal Party, members of the Tory Party, the Devonshire Volunteer Force, the entire council, members of the government (the Prime Minister sent his apologies) and almost every local authority organisation, as well as members of the public. During the ceremony businesses in the town closed their shutters out of respect, and blinds were drawn in the houses of private individuals. It is highly unlikely that the passing of any politician today would cause such genuine grief and regret.

Standing with the Albert Clock Tower behind you, look to the right and you will see the Golden Lion pub.

The bust of Charles Sweet Willshire, erected after his death.

Fountain on The Square, erected in memory, C. H. Willshire.

The building to the left of the Golden Lion dates from 1872. Now a fish and chip restaurant, during the Second World War American troops would march every morning and evening to this spot to raise and lower their flag, which was attached to the wall. Local people at the time recall the noise that the marching hobnail boots would make as they marched by.

The eighteenth-century Golden Lion Tap itself once provided accommodation and refreshments for the servants of those staying at the Golden Lion just around the corner at No. 62 Boutport Street. This is now a restaurant, and was built as a merchant's house in the early seventeenth century, but around 1760 it became the Golden Lion coaching inn. Fortunately, the magnificent plaster ceiling has been preserved from the original house and can still be seen, although the building has also accommodated a bank and building society before becoming a restaurant.

Next door is the Royal and Fortescue Hotel. From around 1780 this was also a coaching inn known as The Fortescue Arms. The Fortescues have long been prominent local landowners, and their arms are still displayed on the front of the hotel.

In 1805, the stagecoach ran three times a week and took fourteen hours to go from Barnstaple to Taunton. The stop at Taunton would be the first on the journey, with no chance of a break before that. The Stagecoach companies were extremely proud of their punctuality, and nothing other than a major disaster would make them stop before the scheduled time. The press of the day would often tell gruesome tales of passengers falling

Early photograph of The Square showing the wide-open space.

Built as a private house, now used as the museum.

from their seats off the roof of the carriage and being left by the roadside to their fate and similar such accounts. By 1830, the time of fourteen hours had been reduced to just eight, although the mail coach would reduce this to five hours.

One of the older prisons in Barnstaple was located on The Square, which J. B. Gribble, the author of *Memorials of Barnstaple*, published in 1830, defined as a disgrace. It had only two rooms, in which up to eight prisoners would be locked up four to a room, 'there to eat, drink and sleep, and preform the offices of nature'. Local people passing by could see the prisoners looking up from the prison. Some would feed the them, while others would taunt them in their distress.

Another prison was built in Albert Place in around 1828 that had seven cells on the ground floor and seven more on the floor above. There was also a room described as 'a debtor's day room and night room'. This second prison only lasted for fifty years before a new one was built on a site near the Cattle Market in 1874. This prison was also sometimes used as an isolation hospital when required.

Cross the road and begin to walk up High Street.

4. The High Street, South End and Boutport Street

On the corner of High Street and Boutport Street you will notice the Youings shop building. This business began trading in Barnstaple in 1884, but acquired the present site in 1934 when the present building was constructed in the then very modern Art Deco style, replacing several older buildings, including a dispensing chemist.

If you wished to continue along Boutport Street, near the end is a building called The Priory and, around the corner of Coronation Street, Priory Cottage. These names are another instance of where nothing remains of a significant institution except a name.

The priory of St Mary Magdalene was founded around 1107 by Juhel – the first Norman lord of Barnstaple to live at the castle. It was a Cluniac foundation originally subordinate

to St Martin-des-Champs in Paris. The priory survived until Henry VIII's reformation, when it was closed down along with all the other religious foundations in England. At that time, its revenues were estimated at £123-6-7 per annum, and the last prior, Robert Thorn, received an annual pension of £14 for life.

DID YOU KNOW THAT...?

The Athenaeum was informally opened to the public in August 1888 following a meeting attended by Mr Rock. He was determined that it was used for educational purposes saying 'he wished the Athenaeum to be a study and not a lounge'. He rejected the idea of a separate room for ladies, as he insisted that for the purpose of studying lady students could mix with male students. He also asked that special care would be taken to ensure that the young men and women employed in the business establishments of the town were provided with 'excellent opportunities of mental improvement'.

All the priory buildings have disappeared, although Priory Cottage and one or two other buildings may incorporate masonry and other features. Extensive ruins were uncovered in 1819 when a tannery and Rackfield Cottages were built. In his *Memorials of Barnstaple* Gribble quotes from an article in the *Gentleman's Magazine* of 1826, which makes a statement of how the workmen employed in 1819 forming a tan-yard on the site of the old priory:

laid open the foundations of many extensive walls, thick and formed of very solid masonry ... amongst the rubbish were fragments of columns, ribs of groins, paving tiles glazed with a flower-de-luce on them, and some stones with crosses ... the whole of these foundations and rubbish had been covered for ages by a fine green sward, and now being only partly uncovered, and the rubbish again thrown back, as suited the convenience of the workmen; it was not possible to form a correct idea either of the extent or form of these buildings.

It goes on to report the finding of two skeletons and some coins, and mentions a tradition that a stone coffin had been found containing the body of a man in complete armour. Gribble also mentions that large quantities of bones had, at different times, been dug up at Rackfield on the priory site. He suggests it was possibly a burial site for plague victims.

In 1830 there was a house on the site, built in 1822 and occupied by Thomas Palmer Ackland.

Opposite: American troops marched here every morning during the war.

When it was established, the priory occupied an area outside the North Gate bounded approximately by the present-day Charles Street, Vicarage Street and the River Yeo.

Religious foundations were very important in medieval times; they owned property and took part in commercial activities. The Barnstaple priory was entitled to payments from the townspeople for grinding corn at its mill until 1328, when the claim was released by a deed between the Prior of the Monastery of St Mary Magdalene of Barnstaple and the monks to the Mayor and Commonalty of Barnstaple.

A possible early mention of the Gorwill area of Barnstaple comes in a request of 1378 by Peter de Gorewylle for confirmation of letters of manumission granted to him by Capiaco, lately Prior of Barnstaple. The names of several priors are recorded including John Ilfrecomb – a monk at the priory who was appointed on the death of the previous prior, John Pylton in 1472. The names seem to indicate that they were local men.

Right: The ornate upper story of the old National Provincial Bank.

Opposite above: The Priory, Boutport Street.

Opposite below: Once the Assembly Rooms, Boutport Street, now the Conservative club.

The Barnstaple priory owned land in Boutport (before it was called Boutport Street) and Pilton. In 1339, the priory of Pilton agreed to grant the rent of Bradiford to the Priory of Barnstaple in exchange for land in Pilton. Relations between the two priories did not always run smoothly. William Worcester was Prior at Pilton between 1434 and 1446. Soon after his appointment he was in dispute with the Priory of Barnstaple over the collection of tithes on land that he claimed belonged to Pilton. The Bishop of Exeter made a visitation in 1435 and invited several elderly parishioners about the matter. He then decided in favour of Pilton, but gave both parties to the dispute ten marks to encourage them to agree.

At the Dissolution of the Monasteries, the Barnstaple Priory lands came into the ownership of William, Lord Howard and his wife Margaret. They remained in the Howard family until the early seventeenth century when they were sold in pieces. Most of the Pilton property went to George Rolle, whose family had acquired the Pilton Priory lands at the Dissolution. The Rolle family retained some of the land for centuries, including that at Pottington, which is why Barnstaple now has a Rolle Quay and a Rolle Street.

One of the properties granted by Sir William Howard, Lord Howard of Effingham, in 1611 for a lease of 2,000 years consisted of two messuages and a parcel of waste ground near the North gate, which abutted on 'a lane called the greene lane'. The property was granted to Thomas Tawton, a tanner whose widowed mother already occupied the property. It also granted the tanner 12 feet in length and the whole river in breadth of the 'river or water called the North Yeo lying and being within the parish of Barnstaple to hang and wash skins and cloths in ...' The amount paid for the lease was £40 and a rent of one rose at the feast of the Nativity of John the Baptist 'if the same be lawfully

The south end of the High Street.

demanded'. By the eighteenth century the property had become the Green Dragon Inn, which it remained for many years.

As well as the priory there may have been Augustinian friars in the town. Gribble notes that a grant was made by Sir James de Audley in 1348 of 'an area in Barnstaple for poor brethren hermits of the order of St Augustine', and that shortly after Robert Rowe gave 5 acres of land in Barnstaple to the said hermits. There do not seem to be any further references to the hermits, so perhaps they never actually settled in the town, although in a talk on Barnstaple Street names in the 1940s, one local historian stated that there was mention of a Friars' Close in 1397, but it could be traced no further. Perhaps this is an instance where even the name has disappeared.

The Assembly Rooms in Boutport Street (now the Conservative Club) were opened in 1800. They were financed by subscription, and any profit was put towards improvements. There were major alterations in 1827 when the whole of the first floor was taken down and rebuilt. The projecting portico at the front was replaced by what the local paper referred to as, 'a neat and modern frontispiece'. In October 1828 it was said the ballroom had lately been splendidly fitted up and was much admired.

In his 1830 book, Gribble stated that the ballroom was 27 feet by 47 feet, with three cut-glass chandeliers. There were two card rooms, a billiard room, a newsroom supplied with two London daily papers, three provincial papers and the army and navy lists, together with dressing and cloakrooms. There were three card clubs held at the Assembly Rooms weekly –two for gentlemen and one for ladies.

There was a ball every year during the fair, and usually one at Christmas. In 1840 there was a grand fancy-dress ball on 29 December, with proceeds going towards the funds of

Boutport
Street –
one of the
oldest in
Barnstaple.

the North Devon Infirmary and the dispensary. Ladies' tickets were 4s and Gentlemens' tickets 5s 6d, with refreshments included. Dancing was to commence at precisely nine o'clock. Many events were held to raise funds for the Infirmary. A ball had been held in April 1828, with guests including Countess Fortescue, the Ladies Eleanor and Elizabeth Fortescue, Lord and Lady Clinton, Sir R. P. Wrey and Lady Wrey, Sir A. Chichester and Lewis W. Buck, MP, and his daughter. The *Exeter and Plymouth Gazette* reported that the ball 'was supported till a late hour in a manner highly gratifying to the brilliant assembly'. The net proceeds for the infirmary were around £40.

Dancing classes were also held at the Assembly Rooms. On 10 July 1834, Mr F. W. Huet, professor of music and dancing, placed an advertisement in the *North Devon Journal* to announce that his academy would reopen on 16 July, and it stated how he taught dancing:

> on the most improved principles in a new, easy and comprehensive manner ... It was possible to learn, 'Genuine Quadrilles, Waltzing, Minuets, Gavottes, Mazourk's Gallopades, and every other description of fashionable dancing requisite for genteel society, expeditiously taught ...

As well as dancing, the Assembly Rooms were used for all sorts of exhibitions and entertainments, and even for sales. In February 1833, J. Ormond notified the inhabitants of Barnstaple and its vicinity that the extensive gallery of paintings advertised for sale by auction on 6 February would be delayed by a day on account of their non-arrival 'by the neglect of the carriers'.

In the era before cinema and television, entertainments were often based on real events. In December 1827, the Assembly Rooms, 'which are elegantly fitted up for the purpose',

Boutport Street. 'Boutport' simply means 'about the port' or wall.

were occupied by 'the Grand Peristephic or Moving Panorama, of the Bombardment of Algiers ...' It had already been shown in London for eighteen months and consisted of nine different views printed on upwards of 16,000 sq feet of canvas, accompanied by a military band. The entrance fee was 2s to the saloon and 1s to the amphitheatre, with schools admitted at half-price to the saloon. The real bombardment of Algiers had happened on 27 August 1816, when an Anglo-Dutch fleet bombarded the ships and harbour defences. Their objective was achieved and over 1,000 Christian slaves were liberated.

Science was another source of education and entertainment. In 1837, a course of five lectures were held in the Assembly Rooms 'to exhibit a general view of those Phenomena of Nature which are of the most preminent interest'. The advertisement stated that the explanations 'will be given in a language destitute of technicalities ... and will be illustrated by geological sketches, drawings of antediluvian monsters, and about one hundred experiments in chemistry, magnetism, electricity and electro-magnetism'. Lectures included, 'Combustion, the Safety Lamp, Meteoric Stones, etc' and, 'Geology and on the Growth of Plants and Animals'. The lectures were given over five days in April, twice a day, once at 12.30 p.m. and once at 7.30 p.m. Tickets cost 10s for the course, or individual lectures were costed at 2s, with reductions for those under sixteen years of age.

The Assembly Rooms were obviously well used, and there was plenty going on in Barnstaple for those with sufficient time and money to attend.

Returning back to the Royal and Fortescue end of Boutport Street; where it joins into High Street, turn past Youings tobacconist and sweet shop and continue up the High Street. Just around the corner look up above the charity shop and notice the plaque, which marks the site of the old South Gate, a portion of which can still be seen behind a door

Opened in 1888 as the Victoria Temperance Hotel, High Street.

The Three Tuns public house, High Street – now Pizza Express.

DID YOU KNOW THAT...?

In the *London Gazette* for December 1772, it was reported that on 13 December the *Susannah*, which carried around 500 tons burden, bound from Surinam to Amsterdam, was 'driven on the Rocks near Barnstaple in the County of Devon, where she was totally lost, together with the greatest part of her Cargo ... She had been carrying sugar, coffee, cotton and cocoa'.

in Youings. High Street was once the most important entrance into the town. In early Barnstaple there was a wall around the town with four gates at the entrance, two of which survived into the nineteenth century, but the South Gate disappeared a few centuries before that. This end of High Street was known as Southgate Street, just as the other end was once called Northgate Street.

DID YOU KNOW THAT...?

In 1695, the *Jeremiah* of Barnstaple took 20 dozen of earthenware direct to Jamaica for John Christmas. North Devon pottery was reaching there before that date by one route or another, as fragments have been found by archaeologists investigating the site of Port Royal, which disappeared in an earthquake in 1692. Port Royal had been an important centre for trade in all sorts of goods. In 1683, the *Fyall Merchant* brought sugar, molasses and lemons back from Jamaica.

5. Paternoster Row

A short way further on you will see a narrow, cobbled path leading off High Street to the right. Turn down this path, known as Alms Lane and now Church Lane, which leads into the old churchyard. Just before you turn the corner you will see the Old School café, housed in the building where in the seventeenth-century Alice Horwood established a free school for twenty poor girls. The girls would have received a fairly basic education, consisting mainly of learning to knit and sew (one task they were expected to do was sew the uniforms for the boys at Blue Coat School nearby). They were also taught to read but not to write, as this was considered unnecessary for girls who would only ever need to read their masters' or husbands' written instructions, with no need to ever reply.

Next to this are a group of almshouses, part of which were began by Alice Horwood's husband and completed by her after his death. Thomas Harrison and Gilbert and Elizabeth Paige were responsible for the remainder of these almshouses, a reminder that before the Welfare State the wealthier members of the local community were expected to provide for the less fortunate.

As you emerge from Church Lane looking to the right you will see St Anne's chapel (now St Anne's Arts and Community Centre). Believed to have been erected during the first half

Paternoster Row looking towards St Peter's church.

of the fourteenth century, it is one of Barnstaple's oldest buildings. The undercroft is the most ancient part and is thought to have been used as a charnel house – a place where bones would be stored when the cemetery was periodically cleared. Later, in around 1550, the porch was added, complete with gargoyles and a parapet.

After the Dissolution of the Monasteries, the chapel was used as a grammar school (the poet and playwright John Gay was educated here), and later by the French Huguenots as a place of worship. Its use as a school finally ended in 1910 when a new grammar school was built in the Newport area. However, St Anne's chapel continues to be one of Barnstaple's most historic and atmospheric buildings.

DID YOU KNOW THAT...?

Juhel died a very old man and was succeeded by Alured, his son or adopted son, but he joined Matilda's supporter, Baldwin de Revers, at Exeter in 1136. and was either killed or banished. King Stephen then gave the barony of Barnstaple to Henry de Tracey. According to a chronicle of Stephen's life, Henry de Tracey 'drew out from Barnstaple, his home town, and made such resolute attacks on William de Mohun's retainers that he not only restrained their plundering inroads, but took 104 horse soldiers in a single encounter'. De Mohun's headquarters were at Dunster Castle.

One of the most successful of the Huguenot families that settled in Barnstaple were the Servants (as they became known in England – they came from the French Servante or St Servan families). They first settled at Bideford, but Henry Servant came to Barnstaple around 1700. He was a goldsmith and established a successful business in the town. He had married another Huguenot, Elizabeth de Bary, and they had several children, who all received bequests when Henry died in 1738. His son Henry received £10, having already been given £100 to set up his trade. Another son received £22-10-00, having already been given a one-eighth share in the ship *Henry and Elizabeth*. A third son, Stephen, received £110 and his father's working tools. He also provided for his four daughters and granddaughter.

Almost fifty years after Henry's death, his unmarried daughter, Susanna, died. She left bequests to several nieces and nephews, as well as £100 to her brother, Stephen. One of her nieces, Sarah Servant, received all her 'wearing apparel', except for one gown and her mother's wedding gown, which went to another niece's daughter.

By that time the Huguenots had become integrated into Barnstaple society, and one of their nieces had married a tallow chandler of the town. John Servant was mayor in 1793 and William Servant in 1802. Matthew Roch, from another Huguenot family, was mayor in 1741 and 1753, and his son, Mounier Roch, in 1760 and 1778. Mounier Roch was one of the founders of the first Barnstaple Bank in 1791.

By the time of Susanna Servant's death, the French services in St Anne's chapel had ceased, but it is sometimes mentioned by earlier Huguenots. In 1722, Michel Soleirol, a

Above left: The tower of St Anne's chapel, added in the 1500s.

Above right: Horwood Almshouses and Alice Horwood's School for Girls, Church Walk.

Left: Interior of St Peter's church, much altered in Victoria's reign.

gentleman, bequeathed £3-3-0 to Mr Roman Alexander – minister of the French church of Barnstaple. He also gave £2-0-0 to the poor belonging to the French church of Barnstaple to be distributed among them. His will was witnessed by Jacob Mounier and Paul Micheau.

In his will, Paul Micheau is described as weaver living in Back Lane, Barnstaple. One of his sons received 'the dwelling house where I live at present', and his daughter, Judith, received 'the dwelling house where my son Stephen now liveth'. A grandson received 'the little tenement behind that where I now live'.

The Huguenots had a reputation for being long-lived. It was said that an old lady, who was the last of the Servant family, died at the age of nearly one hundred, as did a Mr Darney. Gradually their names became anglicised and their French origins forgotten. L'Oiseau became Bird and Roche became Rock or Roach; Le Roy became King and De Moulins became Mullins. It has been suggested that now one-sixth of British people have a Huguenot ancestor.

On your left is the parish church of St Peter. The High Street entrance is guarded by iron gates made at a local foundry and erected in 1829. This was a few years after the demolition of the old guildhall that had occupied the site for centuries.

The ground at the side of the pathways in the churchyard is raised because until 1855 the land was used for burials. Some of the old gravestones can be seen placed against the walls. A sundial dating from 1732 is attached to the church wall, as is a clock made in 1913.

There has been a church on this site for centuries, possible since Anglo-Saxon times. The first recorded vicar of St Peter's was Walter, treasurer of Exeter Cathedral in 1257. However, in the following fifty years, the church must have been rebuilt as the present building was consecrated by Bishop Stapledon of Exeter in 1318, although some masonry in the tower probably dates from around 100 years earlier.

Since then there have been numerous alterations and repairs so that little of that medieval church remains on its original site. Major reconstruction work was undertaken by Sir Gilbert Scott in the second half of the nineteenth century, when the church was found to be urgently in need of work to make it safe, partly because of damage caused by earlier alterations and restorations. By the end of the nineteenth century, the church had been restored, but the interior had been greatly changed.

The twisted spire is a feature of the church clearly visible from the ground. The spire was added in the 1380s, although much repaired since – notably in 1636. It was struck by lightning in 1810, but the twisted appearance probably results from the lead warping in the heat of the sun.

Inside the church there are several monuments, many commemorating members of merchant families from Barnstaple's prosperous times in the late sixteenth and early seventeenth centuries, including Richard Ferris, Thomas Horwood and Richard Beaple. There is also a memorial to Martin Blake and his family. He became vicar of Barnstaple in 1628, but suffered greatly during the Civil War and Commonwealth period when he was twice removed from his position and even imprisoned. He returned as vicar at the Restoration and survived until 1673. He was also linked to the wealthy merchant families, as he had married John Deldridge's daughter, and it was at Delbridge's insistence that he became vicar, against much local opposition. Although three of his children lived to become adults, several died in infancy and are mentioned on the monument.

Above left: One of the magnificent family memorials in St Peter's church.

Above right: Memorial to a wealthy Barnstaple family, St Peter's church.

Left: The magnificent organ made by John Crang, St Peter's church.

Most of Barnstaple's leading inhabitants were supporters of Parliament, and when civil war became inevitable they took steps to defend the town. By January 1643, trenches had been dug and a fort built at what was subsequently known as Fort Hill. Despite these efforts the town spent much of the war under Royalist control, surrendering to the Royalist forces in September 1643. The town had surrendered on terms that allowed it to be free of a garrison, but the townsmen continued to cause trouble and the town was occupied in February 1644.

Although it is not specifically mentioned, the most likely time for a skirmish in Litchdon Street, which may have resulted in bullet holes in the door of the meeting room in the almshouses, is June 1644, when a substantial number of Royalist troops were withdrawn from the town. This gave the town's Parliamentarians the opportunity to rebel and regain control of their town. Although a Royalist force arrived to crush the uprising, the townsmen 'shut the gates against them and slew several of them', forcing the Royalists to retreat. A Parliamentarian force was stationed in the town to help keep the Royalists out, and it has been suggested there were 900 Parliamentary soldiers in the town. However, the town was besieged by Lord Goring's troops and surrendered again to the Royalists on 17 September 1644.

DID YOU KNOW THAT...?

In September 1844, R. Gregory advertised that he was expecting the brig *Nimrod* to arrive from St Petersburg with a cargo of tallow and linseed, 'which he will be enabled to sell on advantageous terms'. He also announced that he had recently received an entire cargo of white and red herrings from the Scotch Fisheries, which he was selling from his stores in Paiges Lane.

In December 1644, Sir Allen Apsley became governor of Barnstaple's Royalist garrison. As with so many other families, the Apsleys were divided in their loyalties. Sir Allen and his brother James were supporters of the King, but their sister, Lucy, was a puritan and supporter of Parliament, married to John Hutchinson, who became the Parliamentary governor of Nottingham Castle. Lucy's sister was married to John Hutchinson's brother. Barnstaple's Parliamentarians were given no further chances to rid themselves of their hated royalist garrison. The town was considered so safe that in June 1645 the Prince of Wales (later Charles II) stayed for a few weeks. The fortunes of war were turning, however, and in April 1646, after being besieged by the Parliamentarians, Sir Allen Apsley surrendered Barnstaple. He was allowed go free, but like all Royalist landowners who wanted to keep their estates he had to compound, that is, agree a fine based on the value of his property. While negotiating with parliament he stayed with his sister and brother-in-law. In her memoirs Lucy Hutchinson tells of how her husband helped her brother defend himself against a malicious allegegation by a Barnstaple woman, who

re lye the Remains of
Lewis Gregory some
ne Mayor of this Town
arson of unblemished
outation who discharged
ery station & Character
Life with the strictest
Probity & Integrity
fond a Husband as affect
arent & as sincere a friend
he age in which he lived
could produce
died June the 26th in the
ar of salvation 1733
he 56 year of his age

Charming headstone
dated 1733, on the
parish church wall.

claimed compensation for a house pulled down during the fortifications. This may have been in Litchdon Street, as it is believed some houses were damaged or pulled down here. It transpired that the house had been destroyed before Sir Allen's time as governor, and that in fact the woman had been a spy for the King and not the fervent parliamentary supporter she claimed to be. No doubt there were many such incidents in the aftermath of the Civil War.

There is also a stained-glass window from 1872, which was installed to celebrate the recovery of the Prince of Wales (later Edward VII) from typhoid – the same illness that killed his father. Queen Victoria, who had feared her eldest son would die of the same disease, paid for parishes all over the country to install these commemorative windows.

Above left: The sundial on the wall of St Peter's church.

Above right: Edward VII window in St Peter's church commemorating his recovery.

The organ was restored more recently, and its quality is such that occasional recitals are given by visiting organists. It was originally presented to the parish church in 1754 by Sir John Amyand, MP for Barnstaple. He was a friend of Handel, who may have recommended the organ builder John Crang. Crang was responsible for maintaining the organ at London's Foundling Hospital for which Handel composed music. During the Victorian alterations to the church, the organ was moved from its original position and damaged. Various repairs were made in the following century, but a major restoration was carried out in the 1990s.

Walk through the small lane between St Peter's church and St Anne's chapel and, before reaching Butcher's Row, look up to your left. You will see a panel set into the brick saying '*Biblotheca Doddrigiana*'. This is the building, completed in 1667, that adjoins the parish church and was built to hold the books given to the town by John Dodderidge, a son of Pentecost Dodderidge. The 114 volumes formed one of the earliest free libraries in the country, although, as it seems the books were theological works in Latin, it is unlikely they were much appreciated. Other books were later added to the library and remained in the building until 1888, when they were transferred to the North Devon Athenaeum. In 1957 they were moved again to Exeter University.

Dodderidge library building completed in 1667 and adjoining the parish church.

DID YOU KNOW THAT...?

The population of Barnstaple at the time the castle was built may have been no more than 350. By the time of its greatest wealth, around 1600, the populace was probably around 2,000, and two hundred years later it had reached 4,000. By 1851, it had doubled again to 8,667. By 1911 it was 14,485 and by 1971 it was 17,342.

6. The Pannier Market and Butcher's Row

Continue past this, and you will find yourself in Butcher's Row. First recommended in 1811, in 1855 a major town improvement scheme took place with the building of the Pannier Market and Butcher's Row. Both were designed by R. D. Gould, and previously markets had been held along part of the High Street. The scheme involved the demolition of a large number of houses, and made use of the site that was previously a slaughterhouse and corn market. The construction of the Pannier Market was not without some controversy, as the size of the planned market was considered too large, with fears of it all turning into an unused white elephant. The area covers the entire length from the High Street to Bouport Street. The Pannier Market, however, was a success from the start and is as busy and thriving as ever today. Unlike so many markets around the country, it has not been totally taken over by the bigger established traders. Local farmers' produce and homemade jams, pickles and pies are still found in abundance on the traditional market days of Tuesday, Friday and Saturday. Every Wednesday the antique market is held, and on Thursdays the craft market takes place.

DID YOU KNOW THAT...?

In July 1942, the American ambassador John G. Winant came to Barnstaple and was made an honorary freeman of the borough. Large crowds gathered to see him, together with his wife, who was presented with a large bouquet of flowers – a gift from the people of Barnstaple. The ceremony at the guildhall was recorded by the BBC for a special broadcast to America. Mrs Winant formally opened a nursery at Pilton, the money for its establishment having come from the people of Barnstable, Massachusetts, 'For the accommodation of British children bombed out of their houses'.

The market opened officially on 2 November 1855, which W. F. Gardiner describes as a 'Red-letter day in the commercial and domestic history of Barnstaple'. *The North Devon Journal* reported on it in detail:

The new covered markets occupy a space equal in area to about 45,000 feet, and extending from the Guildhall in the High Street to Boutport Street, with a nearly parallel width of about 110 feet; the extreme length, including the space under the Guildhall partially used for the purposes of the market, is about 445 feet, the width being about 28 feet. The

Butcher's Market is place on the south side of this carriage way, and comprises thirty-three shops, with a frontage of about ten feet 10 inches each. These form an arcade, the pilasters being formed of Bath stone. The height of each shop is about 14 feet, with the advantage of facing the north. The roof overhangs the footway of the shops about 7 feet, and is supported by brackets, which spring from the caps of the pilasters. The Pannier Marker itself is about 320 feet in length and about 68 feet in width. The roof is entirely wrought, the timbers being visible throughout. The whole of the centre part of the roof is covered with rolled and fluted plate glass, manufactured by Messrs. Chance, of Birmingham. The timbers of the roof will be stained and varnished; and as a relief, the iron work will have a blue colour.

Left: The Pannier Market, built together with Butcher's row.

Opposite: The roof of the Pannier Market showing the ornate ironwork.

The *North Devon Journal* went on to give further details of the opening ceremony and enthusing about the style of the building, it went on to say,

> The style of architecture adopted throughout is Italian, rather of a Palladian character. He works were carried out in a very creditable manner by Messrs. R Gribble, joiner and builder; James Bowden, plasterer; J. Pulsford stone mason; J. S. Clarke, painter and glazier; and Lancey and Sons, plumbers. The whole cost of the works will be between £5,000 and £7,000. The town has derived a great advantage from the removal of the several slaughterhouses, with their attendant nuisances, with formally stood in its centre, diffusing the most deadly and noxious effluvia.

Butcher's Row sold meat exclusively until the Second World War, when the restrictions caused by rationing prompted the council to allow some vegetables and fish shops to be based here, as well as the traditional butchers.

Turn right and walk to the end of Butcher's Row where it joins Boutport Street. On your left notice the Queen's Theatre. Built in 1855 to a design by R.D. Gould, it was originally known as the Music Hall, then changed to the Albert Hall, and had a dual use with the ground floor being a corn market and the first floor the Music Hall.

During the Second World War, large quantities of food was stored here, but disaster struck one night in November 1941, when, after a dance had taken place earlier in the evening, a fire broke out. By morning only the shell of the building still stood. Rebuilt in 1952, the façade remains exactly as originally designed. It was renamed the Queen's Hall, and in the 1990s was called the Queen's Theatre.

Retrace your steps along Butcher's Row until reaching the High Street, where, on the corner of the market is situated Barnstaple's guildhall. This discreet and unobtrusive building is the town's third guildhall, and was built in 1826 to the design of architect Thomas Lee. Lee was born in Barnstaple in 1794, and was the son of Thomas Lee of Barbican House. He was educated at Barnstaple Grammar School and trained as an architect at Sir John Soane's office in London. He was the architect responsible for Barnstaple's guildhall and Arlington Court, as well as Eggesford House and many Devon churches. He had a practice in London and, according to the *North Devon Journal* in its report on his tragic death in September 1834, he was 'rising to eminence in his profession'. For several years he had spent some weeks at Mortehoe in the summer and enjoyed bathing in the sea. In that year his sister and daughter were staying with him. One morning he went swimming when there was a strong wind and the waters were running high. Around an hour after entering the water his body was washed ashore and it appeared that he had been driven onto the rocks by the force of the water. His wife had died around a year previously, but he left a daughter aged around five.

DID YOU KNOW THAT...?

Frederick Richard Lee was born in Barnstaple on 10 June 1798. He joined the army, but left due to weak health and became a professional painter, becoming a Royal Academician in 1838. He exhibited regularly in London until 1870. He painted landscapes, including many scenes of Devon. He lived at Broadgate House, Pilton, but spent much time on his yacht. As well as sailing around Europe he travelled to Africa and Australia. Reporting his departure for Australia and New Zealand when he was over seventy, the *North Devon Journal* referred to him as 'our eminent native artist'. In 2003, one of his paintings fetched £160,650.

Its splendid main chamber had been the town's court room, with many and varied trials having taken place over the years. It ceased to be used in this way when the Civic Centre, built in the late 1960s, took over this task, and its primary use is now that of the main council chamber.

The ground floor had been the police station with two cells, but was converted into the mayor's parlour in 1922. The Dodderidge Room, upstairs next to the main chamber,

The gloved hand put out every fair day.

contains a magnificent, carved early seventeenth-century fireplace rescued from the house of merchant Pentecost Dodderidge, when it was demolished in 1901, together with an impressive collection of Town Plate.

In 1968, plans for redevelopment were being discussed for the centre of town, and at one such meeting the idea was raised to use the Pannier Market site in this scheme. This would involve the demolition of both the market and guildhall, the idea being to replace them with a modern tower block for office use. Letters quickly appeared in the *North Devon Journal Herald* expressing shock at this idea, and the plans were soon dropped.

HIDDEN IN PLAIN SIGHT in the corner of the guildhall is the stone marking the spot from which the turnpike mileage stones take their measurements. It was decided to insert this stone, as well as to provide new granite mileage markers, at a meeting of the Barnstaple Turnpike Trustees in May 1879. They considered it would be a good way of using their surplus funds before handing over to the Highway Board, which would be replacing the Turnpike Trusts. Prior to this, mileage had been measured from different spots in the town and the markers had been wooden posts that were almost decayed. It was resolved that the cost of the work should not exceed £200. There was a suggestion

The Milestone built into the corner of the guildhall.

The poor box dated 1895, built into the guildhall wall.

that the centre stone should be High Cross rather than the guildhall because it was possible that the building might be destroyed in the future. However, the guildhall was favoured because 'as the new milestones were intended to be a memorial of the trustees, it was fitting that they should have for their centre the building in which the meetings of the Trust had been held'.

At the January 1880 meeting it was reported that the milestones and the centre stone had been obtained from Messrs. J. Easton & Son, granite merchants of Exeter. There were 105 milestones, each engraved with the word 'Barum' and a number showing the distance in miles. The old mileposts had been removed. The new milestones on the old road between Bideford and Torrington had the words 'by Bideford' added after 'Barum' in order that 'travellers may not be deceived as to the shorter distance from Barnstaple by other practicable roads'. The cost of the milestones and cornerstone, all lettered, was £83 8s 5d; the cost of gilding the lettering on the cornerstone was 10s.

Walk back into High Street. Looking across the street to the right you will see the timber-framed frontage of the Three Tuns (now Pizza Express). It is one of the oldest surviving buildings in the High Street, with beams and panelling dating from around 1600. The earliest recorded mention of this building was in documents dated 1415, when it was bought for the sum of £8 from John Hunt by a Thomas Walshe. It was much altered in the mid-fifteenth century when the ground floor was a shop or warehouse. Servants sleeping quarters were situated in the backyard. The family lived on the first floor, but by

The guildhall, built in 1826 – Barnstaple's third.

1704 records show that it had ceased to be a family home and instead had become a public house. It was bought by Mr Easton in 1837, when the place would open at 6.00 a.m. In the late 1870s, the famous Fair Ale was brewed here using water drawn from a lead pump in the courtyard for many years. The attractive front is a pastiche created in 1946 by the architect Bruce Oliver. Built as a medieval merchant's house, it had become a public house by the eighteenth century.

Continue down the High Street. Past the Three Tuns on your right stands the department store of Banbury's. This highly successful local department store is still run by the same family and occupies the same site that it did when founded in 1925.

The arrival of the first Belgian refugees at Barnstaple was reported in the *North Devon Journal* on 29 October 1914. It stated that the town had offered to maintain and house thirty refugees; later reports suggested that there were 500 living in the area. There were around 200 in Bideford and others in Braunton, Ilfracombe, Lynton and Combe Martin. One of the properties used to house Belgian refugees in Barnstaple was No. 49 High Street – now occupied by Primark. On 12 November 1914 the local paper reported:

> Sergeant Young (Tavistock) of the Royal North Devon Hussars, can speak Flemish and has consequently been able to render much assistance to the Belgian refugees at Barnstaple, in whom he has manifested a kindly interest. In recognition of his kindness, the refugees at 49, High Street, have presented Sergeant Young with a bugle.

No. 49 High Street, which housed the Belgian refugees in 1914.

Details of some of the refugees were given in the parish church magazine and then printed in the *North Devon Journal* in December 1914. They included:

> August de Saedeleer and Maria Lodevica, his wife – shoemaker at Tirmonde. Their shop was burnt down and they had to flee, having lost everything. Their son and daughter-in-law have been discovered at Bromley in Kent, where, since their arrival there, a little boy had been born ... the party are coming to be with them at 49, High Street.

Another refugee was Alphonse Snauwaert, aged twenty-three, who had been in the Civic Guard at Bruges and was a printer by trade. It was reported that his wife and child were safe in Bruges.

In January 1919, it was reported that very soon all the Belgian refugees in Devon would have been repatriated, and their presence in the area was soon forgotten.

Turn right at the next crossing and walk up Joy Street. The origin of the street name is obscure, but it has been called Joy Street since at least 1578. In the fifteenth century, it was known as Eastgate Street, and if you walk to the top of the street you will see the plaque marking the site of the East Gate. This street is one of the oldest parts of the town, and archaeological excavations have revealed the remains of Anglo-Saxon dwellings here. Until Butcher's Row was constructed in the mid-nineteenth century, Joy Street was the only road connecting High Street and Boutport Street – the road outside the walls of the old town.

Green Lane, just off the High Street.

Rare pottery tiles still in place along Green Lane.

Walking back towards High Street, on the right you will pass the narrow Green Lane, which now leads into the modern Green Lane Shopping Centre, but which is an old lane probably marking the line of the boundary walls. The other end of the lane can be seen at the end of High Street.

Returning to the High Street, you will pass another plaque at the end of Joy Street marking the site where it is thought John Gay, author of *The Beggar's Opera*, was born in 1685. The Gay family had been established in the town for a very long time, and had provided two mayors as well as Grace Beaple, who was a Gay by birth. There were several branches of the family both in the town and outside, most of them engaged in trade. His parents both died when he was a child and he was brought up by his uncles. After receiving and then abandoning an apprenticeship to a silk mercer, John Gay joined the literary life of London, becoming part of the circle around Alexander Pope and Jonathan Swift. For a short time he was secretary to the elderly Duchess of Monmouth, and later became a commissioner of the state lottery, which provided him with a regular income. He earned some money from writing, but became wealthy when *The Beggar's Opera*, first

The Blue Coat School clock, on the wall of the guildhall.

performed on 29 January 1728, was successful. Filled with political satire, the sequel *Polly* was banned from public performance, but the printed version sold well and added considerably to his wealth. Unfortunately his health was never good, and, falling ill with a sudden fever in December 1732, he died three days later. He was buried in Westminster Abbey 'with great pomp and solemnity'.

Cross to the other side of High Street. Continue until you reach the entrance to Gammon Lane on the left. Before turning down here, notice the ornate building on your left. This was built in 1887 as The Victorian Temperance Hotel.

7. Tuly Street and The Castle

Turn right down into Gammon Walk (previously Gammon Lane) and at the end you will find Tuly Street, with the ancient castle mound and modern library facing you. This is an old area of the town, but it has been greatly altered over the years. All the old houses to the right as you emerge from Gammon Walk were demolished, together with many properties in Gammon Lane, when the area was redeveloped in the 1980s. The new library and record office were opened in 1988.

The name of the street is fascinating. The old spelling is 'Tooley', but from the nineteenth century either Tooley, Tulys or Tuly is recorded. In earlier centuries there are also references to properties in or at St Tooley's Well, and this seems to have been the name's origin. There was no St Tooley, but there was a St Olaf, and the well was named after him. This may seem unlikely, but there is a Tooley Street in London that takes its name from St Olave's church – now demolished. St Olaf or Olav was an early king of Norway who tried to convert his people to Christianity and was martyred in 1030, becoming a popular saint in England.

The line of Tuly Street has altered over the centuries. It probably originated in the thirteenth century as a track or 'holloway' along the course of the silted-up bailey ditch.

The library – site of the workhouse and, later, Dornat's factory.

Castle Mound – site of the motte and bailey castle.

Excavations at the library site revealed that it was either much wider than the modern street or that it lay to the west of the present road.

For centuries before this the site was occupied by the town's bridewell – an early form of workhouse. There is documentary evidence of this from the early seventeenth century, but it may have existed much earlier. A document of 1724 ordered 'the officer of the said bridewell or workhouse from time to time to receive and take into his said workhouse such idle and disorderly persons as shall be sent to him and there to punish and sett them at work as the laws direct'.

The occupation of the workhouse masters was usually given as weaver or serge maker and it seems likely the inhabitants were put to work making woollen cloth. For part of its existence the building was also used as a prison as in 1624 it was stated that 'the Prison and the bridewell were under the same roof with one Governor for both'. John Penrose, as well as leaving money for the building of the almshouses in Litchdon Street, also left £200 'to help keep in work in the newly erected house near the castle called the bridewell, the poor'.

In 1657, Nathaniel Hooper leased a plot of land set about with a low wall 120 feet by 44 feet next to the bridewell, with all the stones and rubble there to build houses. It is not known if the houses were an extension to the bridewell or not. A new stone and masonry building was erected in 1792, which was the building eventually taken over by Dornat's.

Library
Square,
Tuly Street.

In the early nineteenth century, the master of the workhouse was the uncle of the painter, J. M. W. Turner, whose father came from South Molton. It is believed that the painter visited his uncle when on a painting tour of the West Country in 1811.

The building's use as a workhouse ended when the new union workhouse was constructed. In December 1835, the *North Devon Journal* carried an advertisement for 'a piece of ground, situate within Three Miles of the Town of Barnstaple, not exceeding Four Acres in extent, for the site of a Workhouse for the BARNSTAPLE UNION'. The site chosen was in Alexandra Road – at that time called Shute Lane. Tenders for the building of the workhouse were invited in May 1836, and by December 1836 the building was being furnished as the Board of Guardian was then inviting tenders to supply 100 iron bedsteads. That building eventually became the Alexandra Hospital when the workhouse system finally ended, and, apart from the chapel, it has now been demolished.

The old Tuly Street building was occupied by a wool combing factory and a brewery before being taken over by Dornat's mineral water works in 1870. Charles Camille Dornat left France in the late 1850s, and in 1860 he set up a mineral water factory, originally on the corner of Holland Street and Paiges Lane. He was a chemist and apothecary as well as an expert on wine, and would dispense medicines stored in soda siphons to local doctors. Speaking several languages, he would sometimes act as an interpreter for foreign visitors to the town. At first the main product of his factory was ginger beer, but other mineral waters were added over time. Despite a serious fire in 1879, the firm prospered and by that year was capable of producing 1,000 bottles a day. Charles Dornat died aged only fifty-one in 1883. His wife had died the year before and their eldest daughter, Annie Hortense, inherited the business. She had married Charles Alfred Youings and they ran

Once the Golden Fleece, now the Fullam restaurant, Tuly Street.

the business together. The firm stayed in the family until it closed when Richard Youings retired in 1980.

The site contained a well, which was said never to run dry, but other wells have been found in the area. The exact whereabouts of St Olaf's well are not known. A fire in 1879 destroyed much of the old building, leaving little evidence of its early life.

In the redevelopment of the area a lane vanished. It ran parallel to Tuly Street on the other side of the bridewell buildings and was known as Potters Lane, although it was also called Castle Lane. It was used by the potters to taken their goods down to Potter's Quay on the River Yeo.

By the seventeenth century, pottery was one of Barnstaple's chief exports, and there were several potters working in this area including John and George Beare, John Coulscot and William Oliver. Excavations in the Potters Lane area before the new library was built revealed the remains of three seventeenth-century kilns, two of which were backfilled and remain under the library car park. The third kiln was removed, reconstructed and put on display at the museum. Most of the pottery remains found were everyday wares such as bowls, jugs and clay pipes, but there were also tiles, tankards, candlestick bases and a ceramic flat iron. The potters' working areas were part of the old castle ditches, which had silted up and were leased out by the Chichesters who were lords of the castle manor. In 1629, another potter, Peter Takell, was in debt to Dame Mary Chichester for the sum of 7 nobles (a noble being 6s 8d), presumably for his rent. He had agreed to settle an earlier debt in kind with 'good tobacko-pipes at 9d a gross'. He was probably the first tobacco-pipe maker in Barnstaple.

Archaeological excavations in the area around the old bridewell also revealed a number of features that suggested there had been a bell-founding operation in the area in the late seventeenth or early eighteenth century, but no details of this have come to light.

The terracotta reliefs above the Squire and Son building.

Rolle Quay docks – once a thriving working dock area.

This area was, however, occupied long before the bridewell and the potters. It is even possible it was occupied before the main settlement of Barnstaple. Earlier archaeological excavations in the 1970s revealed prehistoric worked flints, so it is even possible there was a prehistoric community here. Those excavations took place in the grounds of the house known as The Castle before its demolition in 1976. The house had been built in the part of the old bailey of the castle that went down to the river, and was originally surrounded by a rampart and ditch or moat.

An extensive Anglo-Saxon cemetery was discovered underneath the bailey bank. The remains of men, women and children were discovered in 105 graves, although there had been much disturbance of the ground in the years since the burials. They appear to have been Christian burials, and it is likely there was a church nearby, but no conclusive evidence was found.

The excavation of the moat shows that it appeared to have linked the rivers Taw and Yeo, and there may have been tidal access. There was no road around the site, and the land adjoining the rivers would have been marsh covered by the river at high tide. It has been suggested that the bailey of the castle may have extended as far as Holland Street over what is now the cattle market car park, but no excavations have been carried out in that area.

The site of North Gate House, demolished in 1966.

The date of the castle that once stood on top of the castle mound is unknown. There is no documentary evidence until the early twelfth century, when it belonged to Juhel or Judhel de Totnes. He is the first Norman lord of the town known to have lived here, and it is possible he was the castle builder, or he may have taken over an earlier, possibly timber, castle erected in the years after the Norman Conquest. Medieval documents refer to various buildings on the castle site, including a domestic hall and chamber, a kitchen and a chapel. It is possible the hall, chamber and kitchen may have been within the circular tower, or donjon, as they are said to have been on top of the motte or mound. The castle defences were reduced in height in 1228 on the orders of Henry III, and by the end of the century it was in disrepair. By 1500 it was in ruins and the outer bailey and ditch were sold. Writing in around 1543, John Leland said, 'there be manifest ruins of a great Castelle at the north-west side of the towne a little beneath the towne bridge and a peace of the dungeon yet standeth'. The 'dungeon' he refers to would have been the donjon or central keep of the castle. In December 1601, the town clerk recorded in his diary that part of the castle wall was blown down and blown into the castle, but there was no harm done except to two ravens that were found dead.

For centuries the castle grounds were the town's green space and recreational area. It was open to the public with a footpath running through it. The town's militia exercised there and archery also took place. Bonfires were lit on top of the mound at times of celebration and children played in the vicinity, rolling down the treeless mound. In March 1591, the Assizes were held in Barnstaple because there was plague in Exeter. Some of the prisoners were kept on Castle Green, probably in tents, and the gibbet was set up there. Eighteen prisoners were hanged.

Bear Street. The earliest recorded spelling was Barrestret in 1394.

These activities were briefly interrupted during the Civil War when the castle was refortified. Expenses of £660 were claimed for 'fortifying the castle, building three defensible gates and making sixteen platforms'. Even before the outbreak of war in 1642, there were arms and ammunition stored at the castle. The 'sixteen platforms' mentioned would have been for guns and may have been on top the mound or cut into the sloping sides. Its main function would have been to protect the town from an attack by sea. In 1643, the town itself provisioned and furnished two ships 'to keep the port' and a man-of-war was set forth, mounted with six guns. This man-of-war fell into the possession of whichever side held the town and was captured at sea in 1646.

It was said that Barnstaple was 'made very strong, for there is a Castle at one end of the Towne and an exceeding strong Fort on the other; so that the Towne is not to be entered until one or both the other be reduced'. The 'exceeding strong Fort' has disappeared, but a reminder of it survives in the names Fort Street and Fort Hill.

The Civil War saw the last of the castle's military history. In the early eighteenth century, Sir Arthur Chichester granted a lease and the area became private property until the borough bought it in 1927, using the Castle House as council offices.

Plaque commemorating the site of Blue Coat School.

DID YOU KNOW THAT...?

William Phillip Hiern, the last private owner of Castle House, died in November 1925. He is now almost forgotten, but he was a well-known figure in public life in the area. He had family connections here, as his father had lived in Castle House and his grandmother was from the Gay family. A world-famous botanist, he published over forty scholarly works. He was very interested in improving educational opportunities for all, and played a leading part in establishing the new grammar school, for girls as well as boys.

That house was built in the nineteenth century, but a private house was built there in the eighteenth century and the area was no longer a public space, although there was a limekiln there. In 1709, a list of rates paid for the reparation of the parish church records that Mrs Standish was rated at £5 for the Castle House and James Gibbs was rated at £4 for the castle. In 1830, they were together rated at £50. A crime report in the *North Devon Journal* for 1832 noted:

On Friday evening last, between eight and nine o'clock, a man of very suspicious appearance was noticed lurking about the entrance to the lawn of Castle House, in this town...' The servants were alerted and searched the grounds when another man, '... rose up from among the shrubs, leapt over the fence and escaped.

The servants found he had hidden two new silk hats, several caps and a piece of print. It was proved that the hats and caps had been stolen from the shop of Mr Trestain in Joy Street. The man who was first noticed was caught, but it could not be proved that he was connected to the crime. However, he was committed for a week as a vagrant.

Writing of the castle mound in the 1880s, R. W. Cotton, in his book *Civil War in North Devon*, mentions that 'To the present and the preceding generation this oldest relic of antiquity which Barnstaple possesses has been all but lost to sight. Hidden by a dense mass of trees in private grounds, no eye living has seen the uninterrupted outline of the ancient burh or Castle mound.'

For many years there was a wall around much of the green with an entrance gate on Tuly Street. The owner in the late nineteenth century was Mr Hiern and he added greenhouses to his property. He also created a small icehouse in the mound itself, which is probably the origin of the stories about tunnels leading from the mound. There is a door in the mound and spaces inside, but they do not go anywhere and almost certainly are related to the icehouse. He was the last private occupier of the Castle House. [17]

View of Barnstaple
showing it nestled in
a valley.

DID YOU KNOW THAT...?

Until the mid-nineteenth century, cattle (and sheep and pigs) were sold in various streets of the town, including Tuly Street. In 1848, a cattle market was opened there and extended in 1890, and the site included a slaughterhouse. By 1892, the large number of cattle offered for sale as part of the September fair were accommodated there. Opposite the market was the Golden Fleece public house (now a Chinese restaurant), built by the Bridge Trust in the early nineteenth century, where farmers could meet and deals could be made.

8. North Walk, Castle Street and Cross Street

Walk out of the castle green to North Walk and turn left. A few yards to the right is the old town station building. Built in the 1890s when the Barnstaple–Lynton line opened, the original Quay station on the site where the old bus station building now is was too small to take an extra line, so it was moved to Castle Street and renamed Barnstaple Town station. The building itself was kept intact even after the station closed and the line was removed in 1935; even the platform is still in place at the rear of the building. Previously used as a restaurant, its current function is as an extra facility for Pathfields School.

Continue down Castle Street and you will come to the building of the Borough of Barnstaple Electricity Works. This was completed in 1903 and officially opened with great celebration by the mayoress and her daughter pulling the mains switch. At first only eight public lamp posts and some private houses were lit by this new form of power. Closed in 1950, it is now used as offices.

Walk further on to the starting point of Queen Anne's Walk, turn left and walk up Cross Street to rejoin High Street.

Cross Street is the main thoroughfare between the quay and High Street, and, therefore, was an important and very busy street. It is referred to in a deed of 1344 as Crock Street,

The houses in Rolle Street were built in the late 1800s.

Rolle Quay. The River Yeo was once wider and deeper.

2942   BARNSTAPLE TOWN STATION.

Town station, 1898, built to replace the old Quay station.

as it was traditionally where the potters sold their wares. It continued to be called Crock Street until the late seventeenth century, when the selling of pottery there had become a 'nuisance'. The justices made an order empowering them to act against future offenders. The pottery trade had grown considerably during the seventeenth century, and it is easy to imagine that the potters were causing an obstruction and making it difficult to walk up and down the street safely and quickly. In April 1670 when the potter William Oliver was presented to the court, it was recorded that he,

> ... did place certain earthenwares called potts, pans and dishes in the king's highway in Barnstaple aforesaid called Cross Street alias Crock Street and permitted the same to remain in the same street during the space of six hours continuously to the harm of the town and the danger of all the liege subjects of the said king near the dwellings of those who walk between ...

William Oliver was fined 5s. It seems that the potters soon stopped using the street, probably moving to the quay where one soon rented a shop, and others may have laid out their produce on the ground.

The entrance to Cross Street from the quay was for centuries the site of the West Gate – one of four gates in the wall that surrounded Barnstaple in early medieval times. Although the South and East Gate vanished many centuries ago, the North and West Gates survived into the mid-nineteenth century – the West Gate was removed in 1852. As usual there was some opposition to the removal of the archway of the gate and the quay hall, which adjoined it on grounds both of historical interest and of cost. In favour of its removal, one councillor said, 'it would be getting away a great obstruction in the approach to Cross Street'. He did think, however, that £50 was a large sum to spend on it.

The quay hall had originally been the chapel of the merchant guild of St Nicholas, first recorded in 1303 but established long before. It appears there were originally two arches to the West Gate, one of which was stopped up when the chapel was built. After the Reformation the chapel was known as the quay hall and was used for various purposes including a warehouse for imported goods and a store for mariners.

Many of the buildings in Cross Street have seventeenth-century cores, often hidden behind nineteenth and twentieth-century fronts. No. 10, now a solicitor's office, was constructed in 1901 as the town's main post office. The house that was demolished to make way for the new building had been one of the street's grandest houses in the late sixteenth and early seventeenth century. It had been the home of the very successful Dodderidge family. Fortunately, the exotic and impressive overmantel from the house

DID YOU KNOW THAT...?

As well as the large twentieth-century post office, Cross Street was home to two earlier offices. An early room used for the purpose had to be abandoned for Boutport Street, as the sleep of the postmistress and her assistant was being disturbed by the noise from a rowdy public house opposite them. In 1862, the post office returned to Cross Street, but by the end of the century much increased trade meant a larger office was needed. In the 1830s, Barnstaple had just one postman, but by 1902 there were thirteen. These postmen made four daily deliveries in the town.

In June 1743, the general post office offered a reward of £200 to any person who caused to be convicted the thief who knocked the post boy with the Barnstaple mail off his horse and, 'carried off both horse and mail, and several letters for Exeter, London, Bristol and other places'. It happened between 10.00 and 11.00 p.m. at the end of Newport, around a mile from Barnstaple. The assailant was, according to the post boy, 'a thick short man ... and the mare ... was of a dark colour with a white face and a tail somewhat longer than usual'.

was saved and is now in the guildhall, in a room now called the Dodderidge room. The exact date of the overmantel is unknown, but it has an added top section with the initials P D and E D and the date 1617, which probably commemorates the marriage of Pentecost and Elizabeth Dodderidge.

Barnstaple Electricity Works building, Castle Street, now used as offices.

Pentecost Dodderidge was the son of Richard Dodderidge, who came from South Molton but was established in Barnstaple's Holland Street by 1582. He bought three tenements in Cross Street three years later. He was a very successful merchant trading with Spain and Portugal, and he was also involved in the Newfoundland fishing trade. In 1588 he was one of the founding members of the English Guinea Co. and became mayor of Barnstaple a year later. Much of his wealth came from 'prizes' – the ships of hostile countries that were captured at sea. Richard Dodderidge was part owner of the *Prudence*, which as the town clerk, Adam Wyatt, noted in his diary for December 1590, 'arrived the prudence with a price taken on the coast of Guinney having in her iiii chest of gold to the value of xvi thousand pounds & divers chaynes of gold with civet and other things of great value such a price as this was never brought into this port'.

Before the end of 1591 the *Prudence* had returned with two more prizes, and the following year captured another worth £10,000.

Richard Dodderidge's son, Pentecost, was also a merchant and was mayor in 1611, 1627 and 1637. He was also one of the town's MPs on three occasions. He seems to have caused some trouble, as he was fined for letting the gutters and chimneys of this house fall into disrepair, and in 1636, when he was at least sixty-years-old, he was fined for refusing to become captain of the town's trained bands. He concentrated on trade with Spain and

Merchant's house in Cross Street, dated 1635, though possibly older.

Portugal and the Atlantic islands, trading West Country cloth and calfskins for Spanish wool and iron. He was a fervent Parliamentarian, and at the outbreak of Civil War offered to lend £50 towards fortifying the town against the Royalist forces. He died in 1644, bequeathing almost £100 for charitable purposes including £39 for a weekly bread dole in Barnstaple and £30 to help poor weavers.

Another seventeenth-century merchant who lived in Cross Street was Thomas Horwood. His initials can be seen on the front of number seven with the date 1635. The date refers to an extensive rebuilding carried out by Horwood, who leased the property from the corporation. He and his wife, Alice, founded the almshouse in Church Lane, and after his death his widow founded the charity school for girls there. Thomas Horwood's Cross Street house included early-seventeenth century plaster ceilings and a chimney piece, but they were removed. Fireplaces, overmantels and the first floor ceiling were taken to Stafford Barton, Dolton, and two ground floor ceilings were transferred to Shute gatehouse.

Presumably this was the house of Thomas Horwood that, when he had gone to Exeter on corporation business, 'the very same day that he rode away, was broken into and filled with soldiers, who plundered and carried away to the full value of 20 marks' worth of his proper goods'. These were Royalist soldiers during the Civil War who plundered his house despite a promise not to do so.

Paiges Lane, just off Cross Street.

On the opposite side of the street is Lloyds Bank. When it was built in 1881 it only occupied No. 17, but it was extended to include No. 16 in 1902.

Next to the bank is an antiques centre. The building was constructed in 1869–70 as the congregational church, replacing an earlier structure of 1839 and was designed by R. D. Gould and his son. The doorway is divided into two by a pillar, above which an angel holds a scroll carved with the words 'Holy, Holy, Holy is the Lord of Hosts'.

The entrance to Paiges Lane is halfway up the left side of Cross Street and joins Cross Street to Holland Street. It was probably not an original street of the town but has existed since at least the fourteenth century. The line of the street was altered when Marks & Spencer built their extension. Prior to that alteration, an archaeological excavation was carried out in 1977. This produced evidence of a row of stone medieval merchants' cottages. They were built with clay-bonded stone walls, with rubbish pits outside. A stone floor was visible in one building. It is probable that they consisted of ground floor shops or warehouses, with living accommodation above. The remains were dated to 1350–1400, and they were converted into five cottages around 1700.

Although it is assumed the lane's name refers to the Paige family, it was sometimes spelt 'Page', and one local historian suggested it may refer to the pages who served in the households of the wealthy merchants in Cross Street and High Street, which would have had back entrances on to this lane. Some properties still extend from High Street including the Three Tuns (now occupied by Pizza Express), which is believed to have been built as a merchant's house around 1400. In 1829, the sale of a dwelling house was advertised as being 'situated near the High Cross in High Street, Barnstaple together with the garden and stable thereto belonging in Paige Lane'. It has also been suggested that the lane might have been the Roper's Walk, referred to in 1610.

Cross Street, originally known as Crock Street.

Angel decoration above the door, Congregational church, Cross Street.

Whatever the truth of those suggestions, the lane was certainly called 'Elephant Lane' for part of the nineteenth century. That name referred to the Elephant Inn, which was established there before 1837. It seems not to have lasted long, as a deed of 1878 refers to a 'dwellinghouse formerly a Public House called 'the Elephant Inn' situate in Paiges Lane, lately in the occupation of John Seldon, dairyman'. In December 1839, John Parminter, landlord of the Elephant Inn, together with landlords of two other public houses, was fined for keeping open his house 'during the hours of divine service on Sunday'. It was, however, said that their houses were of general good conduct and there were some extenuating features in that particular case, but what these features were is not stated.

Many different occupations have been mentioned in connection with Paiges Lane over the centuries, and the properties have been greatly altered but may still conceal medieval beams and seventeenth-century doors inside their modern frontages.

In 1721/22, a lease was granted to Thomas Palmer, cutler, of 'an old decayed house, 13 ft 6 in broad and 18 ft deep in Page Lane'. The lessee was to rebuild the premises as a house with one room, with a chamber over it and a chimney to both the room and the chamber.

In 1802 a lease refers to 'one messuage or dwellinghouse now converted into stables in Paige Lane'. Gribble, when recording details of Horwood's almshouses in his Memorials of 1830 states that, 'the almshouse people are appointed from the poor of Barnstaple ...

each of them receives five shillings per lunar month and the rent of the stables in Paiges Lane, being two guineas a year, is divided among them at Christmas'.

Other occupants of the lane in the nineteenth century included a gunmaker, a mason, a smith and a pawnbroker. In 1851, James Brannam, the elder brother of the potter Thomas Brannam, lived there.

No. 4 Cross Street, on the corner of Paiges Lane, is a nineteenth-century building incorporating a sixteenth or seventeenth-century house on the Paiges Lane side. The front of the building is another work by R. D. Gould, who rebuilt it in 1859 for Messrs Farleigh, grocers. Other occupants since then include Messrs Radford and Yeo, a dress shop and milliners and, later in the twentieth century, the estate agents Messrs Philllip, Sanders & Stubbs. On the other corner is now a photographic shop, but several different businesses have occupied the premises in recent years. Although the front part of the building is early or mid-seventeenth century, major alterations were carried out in 1909 for the florists W. Furse & Co. At that time, the ground floor ceiling was raised by several feet, the shop remodelled and the shop window installed. The property was later occupied by the Swiss Cafe.

Continue up Cross Street to the area once known as High Cross, where Cross Street meets High Street. John Delbridge owned a house here on the corner, and when he retired to Rumsam he gave his house to be rented out to provide 20s 'to be distributed by churchwardens and overseers of the poor yearly on the 14 December unto twenty such poor families in Barnstaple to each family 12d as the mayor and aldermen ... together with the churchwardens ... nominate and 20s more ... to be distributed in like manner... on the 2 day of May yearly'.

Joy Street, one of the older roads in Barnstaple.

It was at the High Cross on 9 July 1644 that Lt or Capt. Howard was executed by hanging. This was in the middle of the Civil War and his crime was the military one of desertion. He was found guilty of deserting the Parliamentarian army and fighting for the Royalists, and was condemned by a council of war with no appeal. There is some doubt about his name – it could have been Howard, Hayward or Hayword. The Civil War was a very unhappy period for Barnstaple, as elsewhere, and no doubt the inhabitants were glad to return to their usual business of buying and selling.

This area was still referred to as High Cross in the later nineteenth century. An advertisement in the local paper in 1852 for Gregory and Tucker mentions that they have nearly completed their alterations at 'Scotland House, High Cross, Barnstaple'. They were linen drapers who sold a wide range of goods including fabrics, shawls, hats and parasols. Elsewhere they are listed at No. 87 High Street, which is next to the property on the corner of Cross Street. In November 1868, Edward Pratt, pharmaceutical chemist, is advertising 'Dandelion, Camomile and Rhubarb Pills for ... all stomach and liver affections'. His shop was at No. 85 High Street on the Cross Street corner, but he still gives the address as High Cross.

This is where our tour of Barnstaple ends. Here in the town centre the street layout has changed little over the centuries, but the individual buildings have undergone many changes and the occupants and their businesses have changed even more. Over time what was once there is forgotten, and so most of the town's long history becomes secret.

Bibliography

Akers, R. and O. Friend, *The Barnstaple Bridewelland Dornat's Mineral Water Factory* (1991).

Barnstaple Historic Buildings Survey 1985–86

Baxter, Julia and Jonathan Baxter, *Barnstaple Yesterday* (Bristol: H. J. Chard & Sons Publishing, 1980).

Blanchard, Linda (ed.), *Archaeology in Barnstaple 1987–88* (Barnstaple: North Devon District Council).

Christie, Peter and Deborah Gahan, *Barnstaple's Vanished Lace Industry* (Bideford: Edward Gaskell, 1997)

Cotton R.W., *Barnstaple and the Northern Part of Devonshire during the Great Civil War 1642–1646* (British Library Historical Print Editions, 1889).

Cruse, John B., *The Long Bridge of Barnstaple and the Bridge Trust* (Barnstaple: Aycliffe Press Ltd., 1982).

Gardiner, W. F., *Barnstaple 1837–1897* (Barnstaple, 1897).

Grant, Alison, *Atlantic Adventurer: John Delbridge of Barnstaple 1564–1639* (Alison Grant, 1996).

Grant, Alison, *North Devon Pottery* (Devon: Edward Gaskell, 2005).

Gray, Todd, *The Lost Chronicle of Barnstaple 1586-1611* (Exeter: the Devonshire Association, 1998).

Gribble, J. B., *Memorials of Barnstaple* (Barnstaple, 1830).

Homer, Ronald F., *The Stanley E. Thomas Collection of Pewter in the Museum of North Devon, Barnstaple* (The Pewter Society, 1993).

Lamplugh, Lois, *Barnstaple: Town on the Taw* (Chichester: Phillimore & Co., 1983).

Miles, Trevor, *The Excavation of a Saxon Cemetery and Part of the Norman Castle at North Walk, Barnstaple* (Proceedings of Devon Archaeological Society, 1986).

Reed, Margaret, *Pilton: its Past and its People* (Barnstaple: D. H. and M. A. Reed).

Youngs, Joyce, *Tudor Barnstaple: New Life for an Ancient Borough* (Transactions of the Devonshire association, 1989).

Online Sources

www.britishnewspaperarchives.co.uk

www.historyofparliamentonline.org

www.nationalarchives.gov.uk